DIGITAL
MILLIONAIRE
SECRETS

How I Built an 8-Figure Business
Selling My Knowledge Online

DAN HENRY

FOREWORD BY
MYRON GOLDEN Ph.D.

DIGITAL MILLIONAIRE SECRETS

How I Built an 8-Figure Business Selling My
Knowledge Online

Omni Marketing LLC
360 Central Ave. Ste 1170
Saint Petersburg, Florida 33701
GetClients.com

Design by Transcendent Publishing

ISBN: 978-1-7344284-9-0

"Whether you think you can, or you think you can't—you're right."

— *Henry Ford*

CONTENTS

DEDICATION

To my father, Dan, for passing on to me a vibrant personality and being my first teacher of how to tell a great story.

To my mother, Robin, for always investing in me when I was young, even if I seemed to not appreciate it. I did.

To my grandparents, Robert and Geneva, for always reminding me I could have whatever I wanted if I worked hard enough.

To Hilal, for relentlessly supporting me when I got my start. Our marriage may not have worked out, but you gave me the most important thing in my world: our son.

To my son, Bruce. You are not even two years old as I write this, but you have already reminded me why I do what I do. For a time, I seemed to have forgotten. Thank you, Son.

ACKNOWLEDGMENTS

I want to thank all the brilliant entrepreneurs I have learned from and that have helped me get to where I am today.

With extreme gratitude, my thanks goes to Russell Brunson for helping me get my start and introducing me to the wonderful world of selling online. Also, for having enough faith in me to ask me to speak at your events. You are a true class act.

I want to thank Sam Ovens for showing me the power of focus and simplicity. You helped me dig myself out of a hole of unhappiness. (Also for those funny emails you send me.)

A special thanks goes to Myron Golden for not only writing the foreword to this book, but also for showing me better ways to inspire. Thank you.

I want to thank Michael Hauge for going above and beyond to teach me the art of storytelling.

I also want to thank my good friend Dave Britton for constantly reminding me that I can achieve more than just owning a bar. You helped me sell my first successful local business. If it wasn't for you, I would still be announcing shot specials over a cheap microphone.

I want to thank my entire staff—especially Brandon Lewis, Karla Floresse Hoffman, Gary Rennilson, and Ashlyn Brothers. You kept my company running while I locked myself away at home to finish this book. Thank you for believing in this mission.

My thanks goes to Shanda Trofe for guiding me through the process of writing my first book. I don't believe this book would have ever gotten off the ground without you.

I would also like to thank Lori Lynn for agreeing to be the editor of this book and taking extreme care to make sure every single word of this book was finely tuned. Also for staying up late and adding last minute "AHA" moments that came into my head mere hours before going to print. Anyone should consider themselves lucky to have you as an editor. Thank you.

Finally, a very special thanks goes to Alice for tirelessly helping me create, edit, and proofread this book before sending it to the professionals. Also for making sure I didn't say anything stupid, and for pretty much keeping me together at all times.

Most importantly, to you. Thank you for buying this book, and even more for taking the time to read it. Especially the acknowledgments. Who reads the acknowledgements? You, that's who!

FOREWORD

BY MYRON GOLDEN, PH.D.

I have read more business books than I can even begin to remember.

I have attended numerous business development seminars.

I have heard business coaches, experts, and gurus of all kinds.

Some really have answers. Others simply proclaim answers. But all too often, it becomes evident that many of them are, more than anything, "Legends In Their Own Minds."

Dan Henry? He really is an expert, and he really has answers.

I remember the first time I heard Dan Henry speak.

After listening to him for 90 minutes, I realized that he is a real expert who teaches what he knows, not what he *thinks* he knows.

When Dan asked me to write the foreword for this book and sent me the manuscript, I knew that I was reading a very rare book indeed.

There are very few people who have mastered the business skills of sales and marketing, and there are fewer still who have mastered these business skills and can explain what works in simple enough terms to ensure that their readers get it.

Dan is one of those rare author-experts.

Digital Millionaire Secrets is exactly what the title claims it to be. It will teach you how to turn your expertise into your fortune, and it could potentially make you millions of dollars.

If you want to learn how to turn your knowledge into financial freedom, this book may be your best chance to live your dreams.

This book has to be one of the best books I've ever read on the subject of making money online. One of the best things about it is that it was written by someone who went from a standing start to making over $10,000,000 in three years using the internet, combined with a very particular set of marketing and sales skills.

Dan Henry is in one of my coaching programs, and he has already made his fortune in his early thirties, but he is still one of the most coachable people I've ever encountered.

I always tell my coaching clients, "A coach who doesn't have a coach doesn't deserve to be your coach!" Not only does Dan Henry deserve to be your coach—especially if you want to make money online—but if you are coachable, you deserve to be coached by Dan Henry.

The purpose of learning is not "Knowing," as most people think it is, but the purpose of learning is "Mastery."

One of the reasons Dan is so successful—and has been able to help so many others become successful—is that he focuses on mastery first. Then, he stacks the skills that he has mastered to help his students produce an exponential result!

So, if you desire to have a quantum leap in your business growth, then you are holding in your hands the key to growing your income fast.

Dan Henry is the person who can take you by the hand and get you moving toward your financial goals.

If all you want is theory and conjecture, then find someone else. But if you are sick of theories and second-hand information about how to create wealth at an exponential rate of speed, then Dan Henry is truly the teacher you've been looking for.

If you will follow Dan's advice in this book (and have a pen and notepad handy every time you crack it open), it could cut years off of your learning curve!

I want to end this foreword by doing three things. First of all, I want to thank Dan Henry for writing it! Secondly, I want to congratulate you for taking the time to read it! The last thing I want to do in the foreword is to challenge you to put it all into practice. When you do that, you've finally made it over to "The Other Side of Money"!

—Myron Golden, Ph.D.

INTRODUCTION

WHAT IS A
DIGITAL MILLIONAIRE?

It's about 36° outside, and I'm freezing. This is in the state of Florida, where even 40° is unheard of. I scramble to get inside my Uber and close the door.

It's nice and toasty inside the car, but before I can get comfortable, I notice something peculiar about the driver. He's covered in dirt. I ask him if he's okay, and he chuckles and says, "I'm a gold-digger."

"Come again?"

"I hunt for gold, precious metals, and jewelry at the beach," he replies.

Being the curious person I am, I ask him how much money he makes doing such a thing.

"I make an extra $200 or so every week. I find a lot of jewelry on the beach and pawn it. I would make more, but there is so much competition. I know it's not much, but one day I'm going to become a millionaire," he explains.

"A millionaire? How are you going to find that much gold?"

He then proceeds to tell me his elaborate plan. He is going to save up all of the money from his Uber job as well as the couple of hundred dollars a week extra he makes finding gold on the beach. He will then use his savings to purchase land in Alaska.

Apparently, there is plenty of land in Alaska with precious metals and gold just waiting to be found. He plans to purchase the property and put up "no trespassing" signs. Since no one else would be able to search for gold on his property, he would have no competition, and he would be able to keep all the gold for himself!

I scratch my head a little bit, pondering whether or not I should tell him how ridiculous his idea sounds. Instead, I opt to help the man.

So I say, "Let me see if I get this straight. You already make a couple hundred extra bucks a week searching for gold on the beach, right?"

He replies, "Yes. I use my metal detector about two hours per night, and you wouldn't believe the valuable stones and lost jewelry I find!"

So I reply, "Okay. If I could tell you a much easier and faster way to become a millionaire, one that does not require you to spend hundreds of thousands of dollars on land in a frigid tundra, would you be interested?"

He then chuckles to himself, half speaking and half laughing. He says, "Well, I suppose so, but you better already be a millionaire if I am to take you seriously!"

At almost that exact moment, we pull up to the destination, which is my 8,000 square-foot, $2 million luxury waterfront home in a private gated yacht club community.

"That's your house?" he asks, his glasses almost falling off his face.

"Yes. Ready to listen?"

The man slowly nods his head, contorting his entire body around like he's in *The Exorcist*, now giving me his full attention.

I proceed to tell him how I'm in the business of selling online education. I tell him he could easily sell an online course teaching people how to make a couple of hundred bucks extra a week searching for gold. In fact, he could make $1 million doing this faster than he could ever do it scouring for gold, let alone saving up for years to buy a piece of land so he could spend even more time scouring for gold.

Plus, he could do it without freezing to death!

He asks, "Is there really that much money in selling information like that?"

"That's how I make my living," I reply.

He looks at me. He looks at my house. He looks back at me and says, "You bought that house from selling information?"

I nod my head.

He looks down at my watch. "You bought that Rolex from that, too?"

"My homes, cars, clothes, vacations, doctor visits for my son, investments for the future, and even the ability to help my parents. All from selling my advice online," I explain.

He gives me a long, hard stare and then asks if he can have my card.

I sort of laugh. The week before, we had just hit $10 million in sales, and I still don't have a business card. So, I explain I only do business online and give him my website address, getclients.com.

He slowly pulls away, makes a U-turn, and creeps past my house at a snail's pace, almost as if to make sure what he's seeing is real.

I never saw that man again. I have no idea if he ever took my advice or how it all panned out for him. I can only hope that he took that advice because it's the same advice I have given to hundreds of my clients and thousands of people that follow me online. This advice has helped countless individuals turn passion into profit and dreams into reality.

If you would like to see some examples of what can be achieved, I've collected screenshots from clients celebrating their success with our program. Visit **DigitalMillionaireSecrets.com/success.**

The fact is, everything is more profitable when you teach it.

If you make $50,000 a year as the owner of a painting company, you can make $500,000 a year teaching other people how to start their own painting company.

If you are a personal trainer making $30,000 a year, you can make $300,000 a year teaching other personal trainers how to get more clients or even just how to get started.

If you lost a bunch of weight after having a baby, you could teach new moms how to lose their baby weight and create a $1 million business from that.

If you wrote a book that people love, you could turn that book into a digital product and charge thousands for it instead of 20 bucks.

If you got perfect grades in college but never really studied much, you could pay off your entire tuition by selling a program on how to hack test-taking.

If you are an immigration lawyer that makes $100,000 a year, you could make 5 to 10 times that teaching an online course on how to get your Green Card.

If you own a marketing agency that gets leads for lawyers, you could create a $1 million business teaching lawyers how to market themselves. In fact, one of our Mastermind clients, Andy, started with us before he even created a course. His program teaches lawyers how to market, and he just passed $1 million in sales.

If you are someone who found a unique way to overcome your struggle with depression and anxiety, you could create a lucrative business teaching other people how to overcome their own anxiety.

Maybe you are a reporter that covers the independent film genre. You could interview several indie film actors, ask specific questions, and sell a program on how to break into the indie film industry. All without being an actor! (Yes, you can sell information provided by other experts.)

Let's say you are a woman who loves yoga, but one day you get a breast augmentation. You realize you can't do the same yoga routine because it's too painful. You even start gaining weight from not working out. So you do research and figure out how to modify your yoga routine, so it isn't painful after surgery. You could create a 6- to 7-figure business teaching women how to do yoga after a breast augmentation.

This is what it means to become a Digital Millionaire.

A Digital Millionaire is someone who has created a 7-figure education business. Even if you only hit 6-figures or just enough to quit your job, it's life-changing. But how?

There are several ways to package information for sale—eBooks, online courses, coaching, software, masterminds, etc.

Here are some specific examples:

> **Online Courses:** This is where you sell a collection of video lessons that teach a particular topic that people can consume at their leisure.

Coaching: This is where you show up to live calls, either one-to-one or group and you coach your students in real time. If you combine this with a course element, you can simply answer questions and help students execute what they have learned. It's typically priced higher than a static online course.

Masterminds: Inner Circle/Masterminds are where you invite a smaller group of people to one or a series of live events or meetings. Between what you teach at the event, and what the networking members receive from being in the mastermind together, the value is beyond what is offered through a course or coaching. You can also hold your mastermind virtually. Even though an in-person mastermind is not technically a digital product, it's sold the same way, and customers often upgrade from a course or coaching to the mastermind. It's typically the highest-ticket-item one offers.

Personally, the vast majority of my fortune has come from selling online courses. However, I've used the same secrets shared in this book to sell high-ticket coaching and masterminds as well.

Online courses specifically are in high demand for a variety of reasons. People love to learn. According to an article in *Forbes*, "online courses made $46 billion in 2017." That same article states that "e-learning will grow to $325 billion by 2025."[1]

Now, you may think that all the "gurus" getting rich are selling "how to make money" courses, but normal, everyday people are profiting from the education industry.

For instance, Rob Percival is a math teacher from England. He has made over $1 million by selling courses on computer programming.

The "Jump Rope Guys" have made millions selling courses on jumping rope. Yes, jumping rope!

The online education industry is growing. It's not a temporary fad, either. No matter what the economy is doing, people will always want to learn new skills.

If you are an expert, coach, author, speaker, educator or just someone that has a skill others would want to learn, why would you want to create a digital product?

Scale and impact.

You cannot scale one-on-one clients or done-for-you work. There are only so many hours in a day. Those business models have a built-in income ceiling.

Plus, you can only impact so many people and spread your message so far when you help one person at a time.

By creating a digital product, you have the potential to reach thousands, not dozens. This will bring you long-term income growth. On top of that, you will gain personal growth as an expert and influencer.

Sadly, many people try to sell online courses and training programs, but as much as 99% don't ever sell a single copy. Most people will take the time to put a product together, but won't invest in learning how to sell their product.

Or worse, many people who have a great message never get started or even try. There are so many people out there with the ability to change others' lives. Unfortunately, they never take that shot and start an education business. This fear comes from not knowing how to begin.

The goal of this book is to share what I have learned that works, and what doesn't.

Before we dive in, you may be wondering why people sell online courses when we have college?

To answer that, I'd like to quote Matt Damon's character Mark Watney (this is from a deleted scene from the movie *The Martian*—yes, I'm one of those movie geeks who watches the deleted scenes and then quotes them in my book):

> "Every human being has a basic instinct: to help each other out. If a hiker gets lost in the mountains, people will coordinate a search. If a train crashes, people will line up to give blood. If an earthquake levels a city, people all over the world will send emergency supplies. This is so fundamentally human that it's found in every culture without exception. Yes, there are assholes who just don't care, but they're massively outnumbered by the people who do."[2]

For as long as humans have existed, those with less experience have learned from those with more experience. Only in recent years have we placed such a high value on diplomas and certifications. But the truth is, if you're just a few steps ahead of someone else, you can profit from sharing your knowledge. You don't need a college degree to do that.

And if we're being honest here, it's time to point out the elephant in the room:

Our formal education system has failed us.

People pay $60,000 with outrageous interest rates to attend a college or university. All the while, learning from people that make $40,000 per year, so they can maybe, in four years, get a job that pays $50,000 per year.

People pay doctors to learn how to lose weight. Yet most of the time, those same doctors are overweight themselves.

People pay technical schools to learn digital marketing from instructors that have never made a single dollar online. We assume that because it's an accredited school, it's okay.

I remember attending the International Academy of Design and Technology in Tampa, Florida. I enrolled to learn audio production. The dean of the school landed the job because of her academic credentials, not her ability to produce music. She had minimal real-world experience. The one time I listened to an album she produced, it sounded like something recorded in a bedroom on a $200 budget. But she has a master's degree, so let's just ignore that, right?

Society has programmed us to think these things are acceptable.

That's why, as course creators, coaches, and consultants, we do what we do.

We have more useful information that we can get out to the masses quicker, with far less investment.

We want to help. It's just what humans do.

How to Use This Book (Ignore Only If You Hate Money)

"**I**'m not coming home tonight, Dad. I hooked up with a hottie from the art department, and I'm staying at her place tonight."

That was the lie I told my father back when I was in college, going for my audio engineering degree. It was toward the end of the day, and my class was almost over. I knew my gas tank was empty, and I hadn't eaten in 10 hours. I lived over an hour from the college, so gas was a significant expense.

My parents paid for my entire college through the Florida Prepaid College Program, but I decided I wanted to go to an expensive art school. So I had to pay the remaining balance as well as my personal expenses all on my own.

At the time, I was editing and mixing songs for $100 apiece trying to pay my way. I didn't want to admit to my father I was going to have to sleep in my car, in the school parking lot, again. I didn't want to admit how much of a failure I was. I didn't want to ask him for more money yet again. So I made up the story of hooking up with a girl just to save face. Sadly, I didn't even know how to talk to a girl at that time, but it was the only thing I could come up with.

After class ended, I had some time to kill. So I decided to do what I did at least twice a week, hang out at the Guitar Center next to the college. It was a great place to chill, drink coffee, and play guitars that I could never afford to buy.

But on this day, something different happened. I ran into a guy that was looking for a new microphone, and I could see the kid at the counter knew nothing about recording. He was just there to work the cash register.

Between being bored and just being the naturally helpful person that I am, I offered him some advice. I had just taken the "Introduction to Recording" class, and while I wasn't the ultimate authority on microphones, I knew a heck of a lot more than your average person.

So I explained to him exactly which microphone he would need for what he wanted to do, and he was so impressed that he asked if he could pay me to help him learn his home recording software.

I was a little surprised at this, mainly because there were so many other people out there that were experts at this, and I was a novice at best.

But he didn't care, and I knew something that he desperately wanted to know. So I happily took his offer, and we scheduled a time to sit down. He paid me $100 to come over for two hours and just show him what I knew. Because he knew nothing and was so impressed with the session, he asked me to come back again the following week.

The second I left his house, I took that hundred dollars, put some gas in my tank, got some food, and went home.

When I got home, my father asked what happened to the girl. I said, "What girl?"

He gave me this long, weird stare, and I immediately remembered the lie I had previously told him. "Oh, she canceled."

After enduring a painful 20-minute talk from my father about rejection, I decided to retire for the evening, thankfully, in my bed instead of my car.

As I sat on my bed, I thought really, really hard. This was the easiest money I had ever made in my life. All I did was give someone advice and got paid for it! I didn't have to do any physical work, sell a physical product, or build anything. I just had to offer my advice.

So I made a plan. I decided to post ads on Craigslist, offering help with home recording software for $50 per hour. I screen-shared with my clients and helped them learn how to record their music. That's it.

I ended up making about $500-$1,000 extra per week and paid my way through college.

While this alone didn't make me a millionaire, it did show me the beauty of the education business. It taught me what was possible.

Once I got out of college, I sort of forgot about it and went on with my life. I had bigger dreams and didn't want to be stuck doing one-on-one coaching sessions on my computer all day.

Over the next few years, I tried to learn everything I could about making money online and building a business. I had some small wins, but they were short-lived.

I even created my first online course, which ended up being a massive failure. After investing three months of my life and $10,000 into something I thought was going to be my ticket to becoming a millionaire, I only made a handful of sales.

I tried coaching again. While I made some money, it was just enough to pay my bills.

I even tried brick and mortar businesses. I jumped from business to business. I owned a bar, a nightclub, a T-shirt company. I was also a carnie for a year selling airbrush tattoos!

They all did okay, but never great.

Things got so bad at one point that Hilal, my wife at the time, and I got desperate enough to try selling water bottles on the side of the road. I actually spent the last few dollars I had on advertising those water bottles on T-shirts for us to wear, making us human billboards. And, yes, there's photographic proof!

Right after my desperate attempts to make money fast, Hilal gave me the idea to start running ads for local businesses. I learned how to do this years prior when I owned a bar and had to figure out how to promote online to bring new customers in the door.

Before long, I had about a dozen clients, a decent income, and was slowly starting to get out of debt. People started to notice my success (albeit small) and began asking for my advice.

So I started offering coaching, and not only did I make some extra money, but, in the process, I was also able to help some fellow entrepreneurs that were just starting out.

It felt good to begin to catch up on all of my bills from the previous year's business failures.

Finally, I was starting to get back on my feet and things were beginning to look up.

That was until the day I got a letter in the mail that I wouldn't wish on my worst enemy.

All I had to do was glance at the return address: Internal Revenue Service. I just knew that it couldn't be good. Well, it could've been a refund ... but, no, that never happens.

The letter said I owed $250,000 in taxes.

The IRS was auditing the nightclub I used to own and disallowing all my expenses for three full years. I didn't know why they were doing that, but they were doing it anyway. No explanation.

Between running my marketing agency and doing some group coaching for people who wanted to learn what I was doing to generate as much as $10,000/month running ads for local businesses, I was making decent money, but there was no way I could cover $250,000. I had to figure out something fast.

The next night, I fell asleep on my laptop. As I woke up and peeled my face off the trackpad, I saw a link to an article. It told the story of a man that had made over $200,000 by selling an online course.

This got me excited. I kept searching and found multiple articles and interviews about people that made millions selling their knowledge online.

There were tons of other 6- and 7-figure success stories. Baking, skiing, starting a business, losing weight, computer programming, dating advice, even how to juggle!

One guy made $1 million selling a course on how to use Excel. Another made $70,000 per month, teaching people how to record music. Yes, this was very similar to the business I started in college where I was charging a measly 50 bucks an hour for one-on-one coaching. This guy was banking $70,000 per month and never talked to a soul! He wasn't even teaching crazy stuff, just the basics! What did he know that I didn't?

These people were making a killing selling their knowledge online, and at an incredibly high-profit margin since there was no real hard cost.

So what was wrong with me? I had failed so much in this particular industry over the past several years. The last thing I wanted to do was try again.

But this time I had no choice. I knew there was absolutely no other way I could make that much money to pay the IRS that fast.

I knew I could definitely fail as I had before, but if I succeeded, it would solve my problem.

I spent the next 30 days researching everything I could, trying to retrace my steps and not make the same mistakes I had before.

This forced environment led me to a much different result. I almost felt like an animal trapped in a corner. An animal that usually would not attack, but when cornered, would let out its true potential.

Thirty days after I decided to give it a second try, I sat down to launch the product. I was doing a live online presentation (known as a webinar) and only expected to make $10,000 *if* I did every-thing correctly.

I figured if I could send the IRS $10,000, that would get them off my back and allow me some time to make the rest.

However, at the end of that webinar, I didn't make $10,000.

By the time I ended the live broadcast, 48 people had said YES to my $1,000 product.

That's $48,000 in one night.

A week later, I did an encore presentation and made $52,000.

In 30 days, from start to finish, I had made $100,000—that put me almost halfway to my $250,000 goal in just one month.

Over the next five months, I built a small team, and we quickly scaled to $1 million in sales. I was not only able to pay the IRS, but I also now had the money to hire a top-notch tax attorney and get the $250,000 reduced to only $25,000!

It didn't end there. We kept scaling, and to date, my company has sold over $10 million in online courses, coaching, and masterminds.

At this point, you might be thinking, "What the heck did you do that made such a difference?"

How did I go from having mediocre success in the digital product industry (very mediocre) to being an 8-figure earner by selling my advice online?

Well, let me ask you a question.

If I had a small time machine and I was able to send one thing back in time to my younger self, and it was a written manual on how to start, grow, and scale an education business, would you want to get your hands on that manual?

Well, I have good news for you. You're holding it in your hands right now.

That's the exact reason I wrote this book. If I had only 200 pages to tell my younger self exactly how to become a Digital Millionaire faster, this book would be what I would send myself.

But why? It's because I could tell my younger self precisely what to do and what not to do. How to skip the struggle, the experimentation, and the failure. I could have saved myself so much time and suffering.

In this book, you'll see several examples of what I did wrong, including trying to create my entire course before pre-selling it.

Hindsight is 20/20. Imagine if you could leverage hindsight BEFORE the events happened?

That is what this book is about.

Allowing you to leverage my years of failure (and eventual success), so you can do it much faster than I did.

So if you answered YES to the previous question, then I recommend reading this book right now without setting it down. Then, I would reread it.

This book is about hindsight.

The famous poet Roger Zelazny said:

> "To paraphrase Oedipus, Hamlet, Lear, and all those guys, 'I wish I had known this some time ago.'"

Who the Heck is Dan Henry? (And Why Should We Listen to Him?)

N ow, let's fast-forward to today. My name is Dan Henry. I'm the founder of GetClients.com.

I've been honored to win several industry awards, including breaking the record for becoming the fastest Two Comma Club award winner, which is awarded by ClickFunnels to anyone who has made over $1 million in sales within a single funnel using their software. I went from $0 to $1 million in five months. Additionally, I'm a ClickFunnels Dream Car winner and a Top Three Affiliate winner.

I won the 8-Figure Club award (also awarded by ClickFunnels) in 2019 and have been invited to speak on the Funnel Hacking Live stage to an audience of over 5,000.

Voted the #1 Internet Entrepreneur in the Tampa Bay area, and Top 40 Under 40 for Tampa, I've also been featured in *Forbes*, *Entrepreneur Magazine*, *Business Insider,* and more.

How did all of this become possible in just a few short years?

By selling over $10 million worth of my very own digital products.

What do I mean by "digital products"?

Essentially, I sell my advice online. The main products I sell are online courses, high-ticket coaching, and masterminds.

Some people like to call this the "information business." I prefer to call it the "education business." My goal is not simply to supply information but to help people actually take action and use that information to achieve a tangible goal.

In this book, I will break down some of the biggest secrets I've learned while building my education business to over $10 million in sales.

What you will read in this book is universal. It has worked not only for me, but it's also worked for hundreds of people that invested in my premium programs. To see an up-to-date list of client success stories, you can visit **GetClients.com/reviews.**

This business has taken me from struggling to pay my electric bill by delivering pizzas in sub-zero temperatures in the dead of Chicago winter, to being able to enjoy a beautiful and financially-free life on the water in Central Florida. I currently reside near St. Pete Beach, FL, at my waterfront estate. Every penny that made this life possible came from my online business.

That said, if you think you need to be extra smart or have some "gifted talent," think again. Even though my company has earned over 8-figures to date, in the beginning, I was just an average person struggling to get started. Perhaps like you.

Yes, a nobody can most definitely become a somebody.

Most people in the digital product world that make a million dollars (let alone $10 million) get their start by knowing someone.

Usually, they participate in what's known as a "Joint Venture." They find someone already famous with a huge email list and pitch them on their offer. If the list owner agrees, they will then mail their list with the newcomer's offer. In exchange, the list owner gets 50% of sales, and the newcomer gets their start.

The difficult part is networking and getting those connections to even be able to connect with the "already famous" list owner. As they say, "It's not *what* you know, it's *who* you know." This is true in almost any industry. You have to be at the right party, or know the guy that knows the guy that knows the guy.

Unfortunately for me, this never worked out. I was never taken seriously. No one would give me a meeting. I live in a beach town in Florida, not NYC or LA, so there were no parties to attend with famous internet gurus.

Once I realized this, I had to begin learning how to do it all by myself, without help or advantage from a single soul.

Still, I was able to build an 8-figure empire, most of it while sitting on my couch in my boxers, using nothing more than a laptop.

By the time I gained enough of a reputation to begin receiving offers from "other famous gurus," I had already far surpassed most of them. Additionally, the one time I did participate in a joint venture, the profits paled in comparison to my normal everyday sales.

I'm telling you this because I am living proof that ANYONE can do this. If I can build an 8-figure business with no help from anyone, so can you. What you will find in this book is the "self-made" blueprint to making that happen, even if no one else believes in you.

Don't worry. I didn't need them, and neither do you.

WHO THIS BOOK IS FOR

The secrets shared inside this book are not restricted to any one industry, such as making money, health, or dating. I know people that make $50,000+ per month selling programs on how to produce music, how to train your dog, and believe it or not, how to jump rope!

Anyone can build a profitable education business, but here are a few specific examples:

Experts: If you are an expert who wants to make more money and more impact by packaging and selling your knowledge online, this book will help you do just that.

People Who Don't Consider Themselves an Expert: You may not consider yourself an expert. But if you've ever had someone ask for advice, or say, "how do you do _____?" that means you have marketable knowledge you can profit from. You could potentially change the lives of others, even if it's in a small way.

Coaches: If you are a coach who wants to scale your business and impact hundreds or thousands, rather than one at a time, this book will help you do just that.

Authors: If you are an author who wants to turn that $20 book into a thousand-dollar product that sells like wildfire, this book will help you do just that.

Speakers: If you are a speaker who wants to get paid every day, whether you are on stage or not, this book will help you do just that.

Educators: If you are already a teacher who wants to make more money and be your own boss, this book will help you do just that.

Course Creators: If you are a course creator who needs help deciding on a course, getting started, fixing a course that isn't selling, or scaling an existing course, this book will help you do just that.

Agencies: If you run an agency that wants to break away from done-for-you work, and scale your business by teaching rather than working in the trenches, this book will help you do just that.

You can't scale "done-for-you." You CAN scale education.

These are just a few examples. However, there is one more example I will share with you in the next section, the "Non-Expert."

CAN NON-EXPERTS BECOME DIGITAL MILLIONAIRES?

"**H**ow can I possibly profit from a Digital Product if I'm not an expert?"

Of course, anyone that is a true expert can package their knowledge and sell it.

But what about people who are relatively new to a subject? What about people who have no skills or expertise of their own whatsoever?

Good news. Non-experts can become Digital Millionaires, too!

Even if you aren't "the best of the best," as long as you know how to do something someone else wants to do ...

Or know something someone else wants to know ...

That's enough to package into a viable product. You don't have to be the best; you just have to make a promise and deliver—even if that promise is entry-level.

The idea that you must be "the top guy" is a myth.

Look at Tony Robbins.

He doesn't have any life-coaching certifications whatsoever. In fact, the top two life-coaching organizations outright denied him. Yet, he is the highest-paid life coach in the entire world!

Credentials mean nothing. Your ability to help someone means everything!

But what if you don't have any knowledge? Can you sell a product on a subject even if you are not an expert on that subject? Absolutely! It's called "Curation"!

A perfect example is Andrew Warner from Mixergy. Andrew interviews top business people, he then sells access to these interviews for a monthly fee.

Imagine if you interviewed ten attorneys on how to win more personal injury lawsuits. You sit down with ten successful personal injury lawyers, ask some specific questions, and document their answers.

This can become a viable product that a new attorney may purchase. It doesn't matter that you yourself are not an attorney. You still went out and obtained the information they want, you then packaged it into a product that they can consume. That's a business!

So if you're wondering how you're going to sell your knowledge, this book will help you.

If you're wondering if you have enough knowledge to sell, this book will help you.

If you're wondering how you can profit from selling information that is not your own, this book will help you.

Knowledge is power, regardless of who created it.

Strategy vs. Tactics

C hinese General and Philosopher Sun Tzu is known as one of the greatest strategists the world has ever known.

His most famous work is a book called *The Art of War*. This book shares his philosophy on defeating your enemies, dealing with conflict, and how to succeed.

You would think that every entrepreneur in the world would have read this book. Instead, most will listen to a podcast or read a blog post before listening to the greatest strategist of all time.

In one section of the book, Tzu says:

"Strategy without tactics is the slowest route to victory. Tactics without strategy is the noise before defeat."[3]

This means if you carefully plan your strategy, it will take a while, but you will win. If you gloss over that strategy and instead focus on tactics, you will move quicker, but it will ultimately end in defeat.

Yet for some reason, most entrepreneurs like to blame failure on tactics. They accuse software, tools, or platforms as the culprit of failure.

I'm sorry to break the news. Success (or failure) doesn't come from which button you click.

Great tactics frequently change. Great strategy does not.

When I look back at my career from zero to 8-figures, I can tell you with absolute certainty that no matter what tactic, tool, or button I pushed, the same strategy could be applied to different tactics, tools, and buttons.

Think of strategy as a map to a pot of gold.

If you have the map and you know exactly where the gold is, you can plan a route and decide what types of tools you will take.

Do you need to climb up a mountain, or do you need to trudge through the snow?

Do you need boots or running shoes?

Are there dangerous snakes down a trail, or are you crossing a river in a boat with hungry alligators?

Without that map, you would have absolutely no idea what tools to bring or what tactics to use to find that pot of gold.

You could bring every tool you can think of, but without that map, it's highly unlikely you will find your pot of gold.

The goal of this book is to give you strategies that will work today, tomorrow, 10 years from now, and even in the next century.

I can tell you beyond a shadow of a doubt that what software you use or what specific tactic you think is so essential pales in comparison to a proper strategy.

I'll give you one example.

The vast majority of my sales come from my webinar, still to this day.

The majority of online marketers today say that webinars don't work. But that's just an angle to try to sell whatever it is they are pushing. (Half of the time they are still using a webinar, iron-ically.)

I could sit here and tell you that I found a new secret strategy that makes evergreen webinars look silly. Then I reveal to you that it's an "On-Demand Webinar."

It's essentially the same thing, just a minor tactical change.

But at the end of the day, that's not what is truly growing my business.

It's what I SAY in the webinar.

I remember about 10 years ago, I was a "pitch man" selling pots and pans at department stores for a sales company.

I would get on a loudspeaker and offer a free gift (a potato peeler) if people simply came back to my booth at a designated time. They would have to listen to my 20-minute sales presentation, and as long as they stuck around until the end, they would get their free potato peeler.

At the end of the presentation, I would offer them an exclusive discount on the pots and pans. I would sell 15-30 sets per day using this method.

Do you know what this was? It was essentially an in-person webinar: a presentation that someone attends to learn something. At the end, they get a free gift if they stick around and attend the whole thing. They have done this for decades in the timeshare industry.

Strategy: Free gift if they watch a sales presentation.

Tactic: Free breakfast at the golf course for a life insurance seminar.

Tactic: Free cruise if you watch a timeshare presentation.

Tactic: Free webinar on how to do _____.

What makes these things work is WHAT is said and HOW they bring people in the door. NOT whether it's at a breakfast shop or an online meeting.

Your presentation, no matter where it is delivered, works because of what you say and how you make people believe in your product. Not because you press a specific button.

So even though we may discuss some tactics in this book, the strategy shared here works regardless of which tactic you use.

Tzu would assess the battlefield and study enemy forces. He would discover their strengths and weaknesses. He would find out what they were actually capable of bringing to the fight.

He would then decide when the proper time to launch his attack would be. He would pick the best location to launch the attack. Once that strategy was clearly mapped out, his generals would work out the details. They would order their men to use certain weapons, divide into squadrons, etc.

Tzu's focus was not on what weapons the soldiers would carry.

Tzu would create the strategy that won wars.

My advice is this: if you find yourself hung up on what software or what button to click before you have put 10 times more effort into your strategy, you'll soon find out that you are putting your energy into the wrong place.

You cannot use tactics unless you have a well-thought-out strategy, and this book is going to give you just that.

If you want to sell your advice in a way that helps thousands of people and liberates you from ever having a single financial woe again, then embrace the idea of strategy and let go of the burden of tactics.

That said, tactics are still important, but they change.

If you would like to see some more training specifically on tactics, please refer to the bonus section of this book.

We have put together some free training exclusively for those who have purchased this book. This training is up to date and will be updated if and when we find better "tactics."

That way, you can learn the strategies in this book that will last far longer than any one tactic. Plus, you can learn some of the latest tactics we are using and testing in our business.

CRAFTING YOUR

CHOOSING YOUR NICHE

A question I often get is, "What niche should I choose or get into?"

If you're thinking about what niche you should choose, you're already doing it wrong.

It shouldn't be about what niche you choose. It should be about the skills and resources you're passionate about that can also help other people.

Instead of finding what niche is most profitable, ask yourself, "What can I do to help people the most?"

Don't "choose your niche." Find the niche you already have and explore that.

A Word of Caution about Passion:

Don't put 100% weight on passion.

For instance, I am more passionate about playing guitar than I am about online marketing.

I am also more passionate about jiu-jitsu than I am about online marketing.

However, I am only a blue belt in jiu-jitsu and while I'm a pretty good guitar player, I've never been a good guitar teacher. I've always played by ear, so teaching this to others is difficult for me.

However, I am crazy-good at online marketing, and even better at teaching it.

Out of those three, I have a level of passion for all of them, but the things that I have the most passion for are not necessarily the things that I have the best ability to *make an impact* with.

You must make the ethical decision to choose the thing you are most qualified to teach with a reasonable amount of passion that will impact the most people.

If you choose the thing that you're most passionate about, but that's not the thing that you're most equipped to teach, then I believe you're being selfish and you need to think more about the people you can serve and less about what entertains you.

THE CASE FOR CLARITY

"It's a lack of clarity that creates chaos and frustration. Those emotions are poison to any living goal."

— *Steve Maraboli*

If I could summarize how to create a $1 million education business in just one word, it would be "clarity."

Imagine you are enjoying a movie at the theater, and you have to use the bathroom. There's always enough light from the ceiling lights and the screen to get up, navigate your way through the seats to the aisle, walk down the stairs to the ground floor, circle around and go out the ramp leading to the door.

But now imagine that when you decide to use the bathroom, the theater employees shut off all the lights and it's pitch black. Could you find your way past the seats without tripping? Could you walk down the stairs without falling on your face? Could you find the door without stepping into the wall?

Even though there are many obstacles, those lights allow you to see where you are going and make the path clear. The darkness makes the path impossible to navigate.

It's the same way with your business. If your business is clouded in darkness, you'll never be able to see where you're going.

Most digital entrepreneurs have problems with clarity in many aspects of their business.

Their product is not clear, their marketing strategy is not clear, and their employee training is not clear. Their ultimate goal is not clear, even to them!

Yet, we continuously try to take action on goals and plans that are convoluted and vague.

We find ourselves frustrated with why our marketing isn't working. We wonder why our customers are difficult. We get frustrated with refunds and disputes, why employees don't do their job, and why our products simply aren't selling!

I can confidently say that 99% of the time, when I help someone solve a problem in their business, in one way or another, the problem can be boiled down to that one word: clarity.

In the 1990's I remember reading about a Gallup poll that asked American workers to rank the factors that had the strongest influence on their job performance. Of all the factors, there was one factor that beat all others by a landslide:

"I know what is expected of me."

It may seem simple, but most of the time, when employees struggle to do a good job, it's simply because they are not clear on what that job actually is supposed to look like and what's expected of them.

If you'd like to know right now if your business has clarity, then you can simply take "The Dinner Table Test."

Imagine you have a new boyfriend or girlfriend, and you're sitting down to dinner with their parents for the first time.

The father leans over and says, "So, what do you do?"

If you cannot answer that question in one sentence, to a degree where the father knows exactly what you do without having to ask any follow-up questions, then you don't have a clear business.

If your response starts with, "Well, let me tell you a story."

Or, "See, this is how it happened."

Or, "Well, it's kind of complicated to explain."

Then I'm sorry to be the one to deliver the news to you, but your stuff is broken.

Every single person I have coached in business that has constant problems can never tell me what they sell in one sentence.

After hundreds of coaching calls and working with thousands of entrepreneurs, I finally decided to create a way to help people find clarity with just one sentence.

It's called an RMS, or Refined Marketing Statement.

As long as you can complete this one sentence by simply filling in the blanks, your business at its very foundation will have clarity.

In the next chapter, I'll show you how to turn that clarity into a marketing strategy, but for now, let's get a good RMS down.

See if you can complete this statement:

I help _____, achieve _____, without _____, by _____.

Let me give you an example:

Let's say you sell a training for speakers and your specific goal is to show them that they can get paid more by giving up large speaking gigs that don't pay much (or don't pay at all because speakers should be happy to just get on such big stages), and instead shows them how to land niche corporate speaking events. Events where a company will pay $10,000 simply for a speaker to come in and train their staff of 15 to 20 people.

Your RMS could be something like:

I help speakers triple their income without competing for big stages by landing little known high-ticket corporate speaking gigs.

Now I don't care if your boyfriend or girlfriend's father has never spoken on stage a day in his life or even knows anyone that is a speaker. If you say that sentence to him, he'll know exactly what you do.

Sure, he may ask, "What's a high-ticket corporate event?"

But that's a good thing! What you DON'T want is that deer in the headlights look.

The last thing you want when someone asks you how you can help them is for them to say they understand, but their head is cocked to the side the entire time. You know that look you get when you realize deep down they have no idea what you're talking about? Yeah, that's the one!

This can be extremely frustrating because you know that you have value to give; you know you could help someone. But you just have trouble articulating it to your customer, and sometimes even to yourself, what that means and how you will do it.

Let's use another example.

One of my programs is called Sold Out Courses. Here is the RMS for that:

"I help experts, authors, coaches, and online entrepreneurs create a lucrative digital product business without a large following by creating a high-ticket program that sells automatically."

This RMS speaks to people who want to create a successful digital product business. But, think they need to go through the painful process of building a large following. It shows them it can be done without that and on autopilot.

We have another product we are developing right now called 7-Figure Body. The reason for this product is because I went through a rapid weight loss transformation over the past year, where I went from overweight to being decently jacked. (I'm not The Rock by any means, but I look far better than I did!)

Well, my audience started to notice. We kept getting hundreds of comments on our ads and social media posts, asking how I was able to make such a transformation while being so busy with my business.

So my personal trainer and I sat down and mapped out a program. But first, we needed to come up with an RMS.

We wanted to test the waters, so we only completed a partial RMS and worked it into a "sneak peek." We then showed it to our audience to see if there was any interest:

"I help busy entrepreneurs get in shape without sacrificing work time."

We'll flesh out the rest later, but for now, this was enough to see how our audience would respond. Remember, neither of us is a world-renowned fitness expert.

The response was overwhelming. We had thousands of people ask to be on a waiting list or to buy a pre-sale.

But notice, if I would have just said that I can show you how to lose weight, you may dismiss me as not being worthy or credible. I mean, think about it. I'm not a personal trainer. I'm not super jacked or ripped. I'm not a professional bodybuilder or even an athlete.

But I *am* a busy entrepreneur that was able to go from being out of shape to looking pretty decent. For most entrepreneurs that are busy, that's all they want. They simply want to look decent and not overweight; they have no interest in being underwear models.

By making a promise that I can show busy entrepreneurs (much like myself), how to simply get in shape (not be a bodybuilder), and do it without cutting into valuable work time, now we have a product that an overweight entrepreneur will salivate for.

All without me being any sort of authority or expert on weight loss. I achieved a result, with the assistance of my personal trainer. But guess what? He isn't certified. He is a Pro MMA fighter that simply knows how to work out and lose weight quickly for fights.

It doesn't matter that we are not at the top of the food chain in this industry. It doesn't matter that the majority of what we will be teaching comes from my trainer and not from me. What matters (and what makes the product desirable) is clarity.

The market I'm going after knows that this product is for them, and it appeals to their pain points. That's more desirable to this market than a "general weight loss" product made by The Rock's personal trainer.

If you cannot gain or display that level of clarity in one sentence, then you cannot possibly expect your prospects to understand what you sell or whom it's for, let alone be persuaded to buy it.

In the next chapter, I'll show you how to take this clarity to the next level and not only understand what your product is about but exactly how to sell it.

"Having knowledge but lacking the power to express it clearly, is no better than never having any ideas at all."

— Pericles

Your Entire Marketing Strategy in One Sentence

What if you could create a blueprint for your entire marketing strategy in just ONE sentence?

That's right, all you have to do is complete this one sentence, and you will never struggle to create a webinar, sales presentation, paid ad, email copy, website copy, etc.

Yes, the RMS from the previous chapter will help you understand what you sell, whom you serve, and how. But how do you expand that RMS into an actual marketing strategy?

Now that we know whom we help, what we help them do, what we help them avoid, and a vehicle in which we achieve this, we must know how to take all that and map it out into a sellable format.

The following is called the "Big Domino Statement."[4] I learned this one from Russell Brunson.

As popular as Russell has made the "Big Domino Statement," it is one of the most misunderstood marketing strategies in the world. I have coached hundreds of entrepreneurs that sell digital products, and every single one that has trouble marketing their program has misused the Big Domino. If you want to avoid problem after problem, you must master this statement.

The Big Domino goes as follows:

"If I can make _____ believe that _____ is the only way to get _____, and the only way to do that is through _____, then all objections become irrelevant, and they must invest."

It's as simple as that! Just fill in the blanks!

Okay, maybe it's not that simple. Let's take a closer look.

If I can make [Audience] believe that [Path] is the only way to get [Desire], and the only way to do that is through [My Product], then all objections become irrelevant, and they must invest.

Audience = Your market

Path = Your method or plan or new opportunity to achieve a goal

Desire = What they want—their goal

My Product = Your program that helps them execute the path

So, for example:

Audience = Speakers

Path = High-ticket corporate events

Desire = Make money speaking

My Product = High-ticket speaker masterclass

It may seem straight-forward, but most people STILL misunderstand this statement.

They think it's just some form of copywriting or pitch. It's not. In fact, you should never show this to your potential customers, or anyone for that matter. The only person that should ever see this is YOU. This is your internal roadmap to your company's marketing strategy.

You see, the secret to selling a digital product is to make people believe two things in a very particular order.

The first thing you must make them believe is the path; the way in which they are going to get what they desire. Then you make them believe that your product is the only way to execute on that path.

Let's use the speaking example again. Try to imagine yourself in the following scenario ...

Let's say you're a speaker, and you want to make more money, but you're just not sure how. You spend all day reaching out to event organizers trying to land gigs on big stages at prestigious events.

Every single time you reach out, you find that it is extremely competitive to land these gigs. You also discover that because these gigs are so big (should you land one), you won't even get paid because the event organizer believes it should be enough simply to let you speak and gain exposure.

So there you are, trying to kick off your speaking career and getting nowhere. Because you believe you should be landing these huge gigs, gaining exposure, and hoping that exposure leads to a paid gig eventually down the road ... maybe.

You don't realize it yet, but you falsely believe that big gigs are the path to a successful speaking career.

But then "The Man in the Red Hat" comes along and shows you a check for $20,000 he received for speaking at one gig for two hours.

The man asks you, "Would you like to learn how to get paid $20,000 per gig? Or even $10,000? Heck, even $5,000?"

Excited, you respond, "Of course! Teach me!"

Now "The Man in the Red Hat" tells you that he used to try to land big gigs, but every time he did, they would never pay because they thought the exposure was enough payment. Additionally, he rarely landed those gigs because they were so competitive.

As you are listening, you begin to relate and empathize with this man, because it's exactly what you are going through.

He then says, "But one day I found out that corporations have a little known thing called an employee training budget."

"This is a set budget they must spend every year on training for their employees. For instance, a car dealership must spend $50,000 per year on training their salespeople to sell more cars and sell more service."

And so "The Man in the Red Hat" explains how he reached out to these corporations, told them he was a sales trainer, and offered to come and train their employees for the low, low fee of $20,000.

He was able to land 10 gigs his very first year, netting him over $200,000 that year in speaking fees.

The secret he shares is that he focused on high-ticket corporate events. He targeted corporations that had a budget for these trainings, showed them that his expertise could help their employees, and closed the deal.

He then goes on to explain how you don't have to be a great salesperson because these corporations HAVE to spend their budget. They are mandated to spend it by the end of the year. So merely by reaching out and asking, you can close way more deals than you think!

At this point, you are completely sold on the fact that you should be going after corporate gigs instead of large general stages.

You now believe the *new* way (landing high-ticket corporate gigs) is better than the *old* way you had been trying (going after big stages).

You feel appreciative that he shared this secret with you, and you've received tons of value!

But you still have tons of questions.

- How do you find these corporations?
- How do you get to the right department?
- How do you know if they've spent their budget or not?
- How do you tailor your speech to their employees?
- How do you accept payment?
- How do you deal with contracts?
- How do you secure a deposit?

How do you make sure your speech is valuable enough to justify the cost, even though they have to spend it anyway?

How do you get invited back next year so you don't have to keep closing new clients, and can instead keep speaking for the same corporations and always have a gig in the pipeline?

You think about these questions and begin asking them one by one...

So, "The Man in the Red Hat," says, "Well, there is a lot to this, and I would love to teach it to you step-by-step. I can coach you, but there will be a fee. However, you can more than pay for that fee with just one gig. In fact, one gig will pay for that fee two to five times over, depending on the gig you land."

Would you be interested? Most would say yes.

But why?

It's because "The Man in the Red Hat" first made you believe that landing corporate events was the only way you're going to make a living as a speaker fast ... and without doing the thing you hate the most: competing over gigs that don't pay.

Then, once you are completely convinced that corporate events are the path to getting what you want, he then convinced you that his program could not only teach you exactly how to execute that plan but would more than pay for itself even if you had moderate success.

You are sold.

You are sold because you were convinced of the plan first, so you bought the thing that allowed you to execute the plan.

If you are not convinced of the path first, the product will have little to no appeal to you.

So let's take a look at that Big Domino Statement if "The Man in the Red Hat" really existed and was actually selling this program.

"If I can make speakers believe that the only way to make $10,000 or more per gig without competing over gigs that don't pay is by focusing on high-ticket corporate events, and the only way to do that is through my high-ticket speaker masterclass, then all objections become irrelevant, and they must invest."

And that, ladies and gentlemen, is how you sell a program.

Whether you're creating a sales video, an email, a webinar, even a live presentation on stage, as long as you always knock over the first domino before you knock over the second, you will always have a clear offer with a clear pitch.

As I said in the previous chapter, clarity is your number one tool for success.

In the next chapter, I'll show you how to make a clear promise to your customers that makes sure people salivate over your product.

THE PROMISE

What is the difference between a program that sells and one that fails?

What's the difference between a product you can sell for $60 and one you can sell for $6,000?

When most people try to create a digital product, coaching program, mastermind, online course, etc., they usually make a very common mistake.

They create a product that doesn't have a QER. That stands for Quantifiable End Result.

A QER means that when your customers complete your program, they will achieve, or have the ability to achieve, a result that is measurable.

People do not spend money on information because they think the information is neat or helpful. They spend it because they have a goal, and they believe that information will help them achieve that goal.

I remember listening to one of my good friends and colleague Ryan Stewman speak at one of my events. Ryan is a world-renowned sales trainer and was talking about how the mortgage officers make the mistake of talking about mortgages instead of talking about the home.

"Nobody wants a mortgage. They want a home."

Mortgage officers that fail regularly talk about low rates, points, etc. Successful mortgage officers keep the conversation focused on the home.

This really resonated with me. Think about it ...

If you're a travel agent, do you talk about the plane ride? Do you tell your potential traveler all the features that the plane has, the food they serve, how the plane was built, why it's such an incredible aircraft?

Or do you tell them about the resort? The vacation destination.

People do not care about the plane. They care about the destination. The resort on that beautiful island they can't wait to sink their toes into.

It's the same with digital products. Most people think about all the features the program will have. How many modules. How many lessons. How long the lessons are. How many cheat sheets. How many coaching calls per week and on and on and on ...

They talk about all these features when deciding on pricing, marketing, how they present the offer. And it's a huge mistake.

What they should be talking about instead is what that information will get them.

If you could choose between a college degree that will teach you how to make more money, and a magic wand you can wave that will instantly deposit $1 million into your bank account, which would you choose?

You would choose the magic wand every time. Why? Because the magic wand gets you what you want the fastest. The college degree may or may not.

But that magic wand, that's a guaranteed win.

Unfortunately, we do not have magic wands. So when selling our programs, we must focus on what that magic wand would do for our customers if it existed.

The easiest way to do this is to deliver a promise, specifically a QER (Quantifiable End Result).

If you were selling a program for speakers, you wouldn't just say the program helps you become a better speaker.

Nobody wants to become a better speaker. They want to wow audiences. They want to get paid more for their speaking. They want to land bigger gigs. They want the things that becoming a better speaker will get them.

So if your promise at the end of your program is to become a better speaker, that's going to be a hard sell.

What's better? Pick a quantifiable end result such as landing your first paid speaking gig, doubling your speaking fees, winning your first highly paid corporate event, or putting together your first demo reel.

That is a much easier sell. Why? Because you have promised something measurable. Something specific that they want.

Now, you may have the urge to try to help everyone. Perhaps you want to help every speaker in the world. Unfortunately, many times when we try to help everyone, we end up reaching no one.

Remember, people don't buy products, they buy solutions.

Every product is an answer to a problem. If you are hungry, you go buy food. If your house is too hot, you buy an AC system. If you are bored, you buy a movie or game.

That's how you must view your education business. You must find a problem and solve it. The more specific the problem, the better.

A speaker that is already at 6-figures does not need to buy a program on landing their first speaking gig. A speaker that has never been paid to speak has little interest in doubling their fees. They just want to land that first gig!

If you pick a particular type of customer with a specific problem, and your product can solve that problem, it's a no brainer. Even if it is a small or entry-level promise, your product will have 100 times higher chance of success.

Plus, when you market your testimonials and client results, it will be much easier to convince new prospective students and clients. You'll be able to share stories of people that achieve that quantifiable end result.

Once you're able to do that, you don't even have to be a great marketer. You simply have to put your results on display. The only way to get those results is to decide on a quantifiable end result and deliver. You can't deliver if your end result is not clear.

If that end result is not clear or undefined, every aspect of building your business will become an uphill battle.

THE OUTLINE

If there is one thing I could impress upon anyone, it's the power of an outline.

I've spent weeks, sometimes even months, working on an outline for a product. Why would I do that? Well, let me tell you a little story.

One time, I sat down to create a new offer that I was really excited about. I was so excited that I just started recording videos and taking action. I recorded all the videos for the entire program in one weekend!

They were all done and ready to go. But, when I sat back and looked at them, I realized something incredibly disturbing.

I had rushed through the process of creation, and I hadn't properly planned. I made some very fundamental mistakes that would have been very bad for the student. I didn't think it through. Thus, the entire product crumbled beneath its own weight.

To ensure I wasn't being too critical on myself, I sent it out to a few colleagues to see what their opinion was. They told me the same thing. They said, "Dan, you're so talented and have made such good products before. What the hell is this? Why did you do it differently?"

I knew right away. I didn't create a blueprint, and I didn't outline the program.

This all reminded me of the time I was angry that I had to pay out $10,000 to an architect. You see, we needed him to create a drawing for a structure we were building. (Yes, I do some real estate investing, but that's a story for another time.)

I thought, why would I have to pay this much money for someone to draw something on a piece of paper? But then I realized that this man had the most important job of anyone when it came to building a structure.

You could have some of the best contractors in the world on the job. But, if the plan is drafted poorly, it simply won't matter. Everything would have been built according to a bad plan, and therefore, it will crumble.

This often happens in the state of Florida, where I live. People shortcut on the planning; they push blueprints through that aren't fully refined. This can cause many problems within the house. Some of which are so bad, it's cheaper to knock the entire house down and rebuild it from scratch.

The same goes for your digital product business. It doesn't matter if it's coaching an online course, mastermind, or even a book. If you don't create the proper blueprint, your product will fail. That is the power of the outline.

I will show you exactly how to outline your product so not only is it successful, but it also produces the result that you have promised. As long as you follow this formula, you should be able to create a digital product that makes sense to your customers and gets them what they want.

Don't worry if it takes you several drafts. Often, I will go through 10 to 20 different versions of my outline before I actually sit down to start recording or producing the product.

I can't stress this enough. The power is in the outline. Create an outline that makes sense. Create a journey for your customers from start to finish, and you will be successful. That said, let's get into the outline.

Below is an illustration of a customer's journey from point A to point B.

You will notice that the first line indicates their current situation. It's where they are right now before the purchase of your product.

The final line at the end indicates where they want to be. This is the promise that your program makes. At the same time, this is a promise your customers would be happy to have fulfilled.

For instance, let's say you're selling a course on speaking, and your target market is new speakers. The first line could be something like, "Never paid to speak," and the final line could be, "Lands first paid speech."

That is an obvious path between where they are now and where they want to be. All your program has to do is get them from point A to point B. It doesn't have to make them the next Tony Robbins or $1 million speaker. It only needs to achieve point A to point B.

Now you'll want to draw several small lines between those two big lines. These small lines should represent the linear milestones (or steps) needed to get from point A to point B. If the student completes each milestone in order, they will likely achieve the desired result the program will promise.

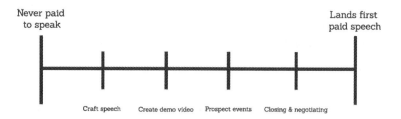

Once you have that down, look at each milestone. Those milestones become your modules. Now ask yourself, "What are the individual details needed to complete this module?" Simply break down the steps in detail. These steps become your lessons.

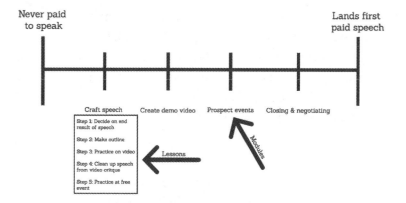

To summarize, the milestones are considered modules, and the steps that make up those milestones are considered the lessons.

If you're preparing for an event, it's the same thing. You're just presenting it live.

If you're doing coaching, it's the same thing. You're just teaching it live.

If you're writing a book, your modules could be your chapter headings and your lessons are the individual steps within each chapter. Do you see what I mean?

If this does not make sense when looking at your outline first, then when you finally sit down to create the content, none of it is going to make sense.

Your customer will be confused, and you will be confused. But, if you have a strong, refined outline, then the process of creating the content will flow easily and smoothly. In fact, whenever I create a strong outline, I find I'm able to produce high-quality content five times faster than if I didn't have a plan of action.

Every time I create a new digital product, I spend far more time on the outline. In fact, the last program I created, I spent more time on the outline than I ever have. The people that bought this particular program had also purchased a lot of my other programs. I've received dozens of emails saying how great the program is! And that it's better than anything they had ever bought on the market.

If someone were to ask me what the number one secret is to creating a successful high-quality digital product, and what has been the biggest needle-mover for me, I would say, creating a strong outline and not taking the next step until you are 100% satisfied with it.

"Give me five minutes to chop down a tree, and I will spend the first two and a half sharpening my axe."

— Unknown Woodsman

HOW TO TEACH

"I never teach my pupils. I only attempt to provide the conditions in which they can learn."

— *Albert Einstein*

When I was a kid, I would always listen to my father, but very rarely listened to my mother. It wasn't because I didn't like or respect her. It was only because my father was better at persuasion and teaching.

I remember I used to go in the cabinets underneath the kitchen sink relentlessly. My mother, who was in the kitchen more often than my father, would say things like, "Daniel, don't go in there." Or, "Stop doing that. Get out of there."

She would always simply tell me not to go in there, without any reasoning as to why. Well, one day, it hit a breaking point, and my mother asked my father to do something about this.

My father came up to me and said, "Son, do you know Jeffrey from down the street?"

And I said, "No."

He replied, "Well, that's probably because Jeffrey died last week. You see, he went under the sink and touched something he shouldn't have. It made him sick, and he died. He was never able to see his parents again, never able to play again. He's dead."

I sat there with my eyes as wide as silver dollars as he told this to me.

He ended with, "So what do you think you should do?"

I remember feeling freaked out by this story. Before I even had time to think, I blurted out, "I shouldn't go under the sink."

My father replied, "That's right."

From that moment on, I never went under the sink again. You see, instead of my father just telling me what to do, he told me a story, which allowed me to come to my own conclusion on what to do.

Have you ever heard the saying, "Make them think it's their idea?"

Well, there's a reason that is so powerful. When someone hears a story that brings them to the conclusion that they must do whatever the principle of that story is, they are much more likely to do it.

Giving steps is not enough. You must inspire them. They have to care enough to take the steps. If you do this, you will not only make more money, but you will also make more impact. More of your students will get results, and thus, you will have more testimonials and more social proof. These things will grow your business even more.

It is not enough that someone gives you money and asks you to teach them. You must continuously inspire that person to do the work.

What I'd like to share with you right now is how I approach teaching.

I've learned this after teaching over 15,000 paying customers how to grow their businesses. I first discovered it from teaching martial arts to children.

Once I started teaching this way, not only did a couple of my students place in national competitions, but I have also helped create quite a few millionaires.

It looks something like this:

State the point of the lesson.

(This lesson is called _____, which will show you how to _____.)

Share a story that illustrates WHY this is important.

(Let me share a story of why it's so important to _____.)

Share the step by step instructions.

(Here is the step by step how to _____.)

Share examples of this lesson put into action.

(One of our other students did this, and their results are _____.)

Re-state the point of the lesson.

(Now you know how to _____.)

That's it! Don't overcomplicate it, but also do not think that you do not need to share some inspiration in each lesson. You do.

It's easy to get someone to pay money to learn something. It's harder to get that same person to take action on what they have learned.

In the next section of this book, we will take a look at your first steps when it comes to asking people to pay you for your advice.

"I am not a teacher, but an awakener."
— Robert Frost

TESTING YOUR

WHY YOU MUST ALWAYS SELL BEFORE YOU CREATE

Wait—what? Sell BEFORE you create? Isn't that unethical?

I've been on hundreds of webinars, countless sales calls, and read thousands of comments from prospects. The number one objecttion I get when I tell someone to sell their program before they create it?

"That's unethical."

I believe people are conditioned to believe it's unethical because of social programming, not because it makes sense. In a moment, I'll show you exactly why it is MORE ethical to pre-sell your program. In fact, selling THEN creating is your best bet of making a product that your students will absolutely love.

Have you ever heard of the famed poet Alexander Pope? In 1713, Pope set out to translate over 15,000 lines of Greek text into English.

This endeavor was a monumental project that would take more than five years, tons of resources, and an enormous amount of money to complete.

Considering the massive expense, Pope wanted to make sure this book would be a success. So he decided to make a pitch to the people.

The pitch was simply this:

If they invested two gold guineas in supporting the effort to make the book, they would get exclusive incentives that no one else would. These incentives included a first edition of the book, their name mentioned in the acknowledgments, and the pleasure of helping to modernize ancient poetry.

750 people took Pope up on his offer, and Pope was able to fund the book.[5]

Do you know what book I'm referring to?

The famous translation of Homer's *Iliad*.

I think it's safe to say in this situation that everyone wins!

Now, let's say you're not big into history or poetry; let me give you another example.

Have you ever heard of Perry Chen?

In 2009, Chen founded a company that the very next year TIME Magazine called one of "The 50 Best Inventions of 2010."[6]

I'll tell you what that company was in a moment.

Perhaps you've heard of it, maybe you haven't, but what's interesting is how it came about.

You see, Chen was always big into the music industry. In 2001 he had an idea to bring a famous pair of DJs down to play a show during the 2002 Jazz Fest. He went through the trouble of finding an excellent venue and reaching out to management. Unfortunately, in the end, the show did not happen due to the lack of funds.

He hated the fact that the people that mattered the most, the audience, had no say.

He thought to himself, "What if people could go to a site and pledge to buy tickets for a show? And if enough money was pledged they would be charged and the show would happen. If not, it wouldn't."[5]

During the next few years, he couldn't get this idea out of the back of his head.

In 2005 he met his future partner, Yancey Strickler. They began working together and brainstorming how to make this idea he had come to life.

They were determined to make this dream a reality and over the next few years, brought in other individuals and partners who were able to help.

They created code, wireframes, and specifications for the website. Finally, it was complete and ready to bring to the world. They had no idea if anyone would even like this idea or if it would work.

The idea for the website was simple.

A creator can upload their idea for a product or project and ask for pre-sales and pledges. If enough people paid before the product/ project was complete, they would create the product. If not, then they did not create the product, and no further work was required.

People that pledged early would get additional incentives that were delivered once the product was complete. Incentives that regular customers, later on, would not receive.

Ten years later, this website has helped fund over 175,000 projects to date (and that number continues to climb), $4.7 billion has been pledged, and over 17 million people have gleefully paid for products yet to be created, thus allowing them to be created *without* cutting corners.[6]

Now they had the funds to make something great and the confidence it would sell.

The name of this website is Kickstarter.

So let me ask you, if it's good enough for Kickstarter (one of the most popular and highly revered startups of the past 50 years), is it good enough for you?

Let me tell you how I apply this to the online education business.

I call this the "Beta Launch."

The first time I tried to create an educational product, I built the whole thing without ever telling anyone what was happening. I recorded all the videos, created all the educational content, and finished the product.

It took me about six months and $10,000 in investment. I bought video cameras, microphones, a green screen—the works.

Well, guess what happened when I launched? Not only did only 12 people buy, which was a massive failure, but those people honestly thought the product wasn't that good.

They weren't contesting that I knew what I was doing. Those that bought knew that I was very good at the subject matter. However, after taking the course, they still didn't get it! Simply put, my curriculum did not explain it well enough. As a result, dozens and dozens of questions came pouring in from students. Even though only a handful bought, I got almost a hundred questions!

This experience caused me to rethink the entire program. Now I had to go back and correct all of these lessons. Plus, I wasn't even getting paid for it! To make matters worse, I only made about $2,400 off a $10,000 investment!

That was the last time I created an information product for about four years. I just didn't think I had it in me, and I thought this was just another failed idea.

Little did I know that I simply went about it all wrong. I let society tell me that it's unethical to sell something before you create it, and I didn't break down the mechanics of what that meant.

Four years after this disaster, I decided to give it another shot. Kickstarter inspired me, so this time I sold the program before I ever created it.

This second attempt was where I first discovered the power of a "Beta Launch."

The pitch was simple. You would get a 50% discount, and I would teach it to you live. Meaning, once the pre-sale was over, about a week later, you would attend a live training where I would teach the curriculum over a streaming broadcast. Then I would take questions after each lesson.

What happened next was quite phenomenal.

I made $12,000 in sales after making this "Beta Pitch," but that's not the best part.

As I was teaching live, if I came to a point where students didn't quite understand something, they let me know right there on the broadcast.

Maybe it was the analogy I used or an example confused them; it could have been anything.

So I would ask at the end of every lesson, "Did you understand this?"

If they said no, I would pause, think of a different way to explain it, and try that. I kept re-explaining things until people said, "Oh, now I get it."

I then took the recordings and edited out the inadequate explanations and left the ones students loved.

Plus, when I went to refine my program and re-record it, I was able to produce an educational curriculum that allowed students to get results without having tons of questions.

This process helped my students because they got bigger, better, and faster results. It also helped me because I no longer had to answer a ton of questions that were simply due to not taking the time to test my curriculum.

Since then, I have taught this process to my clients, which has allowed them to make nearly instant money with very little upfront work! More importantly, it has helped to create *massive* results for their students!

On a side note, all my premium clients learn "The Beta Pitch." This fill-in-the-blanks script is about as close as one can get to yelling, "Abracadabra," and money just appearing before their eyes. (You can find this script in the 30 Days to $100K Blueprint later in this book.)

For instance, one of my clients, Zach, earned $6,237 doing his first Beta Pitch to only 30 people! Another client, Jason, butchered the Beta Pitch and did almost everything wrong, yet he did enough right to make $6,843.

My client Aileen really knocked it out of the park and made $96,000 with her Beta before ever creating her program.

To see screenshots from the above clients, as well as more examples of clients that have succeeded with the Beta Pitch, visit **DigitalMillionaireSecrets.com/beta.**

So there it is. If you sell something before you create it, you have time to refine it and make it great. Your initial group of Beta students will love your product because you've worked with them to refine it. They will feel special.

Finally, your future students will have the best possible version of your product.

However, if you throw something together without testing it or working with students, then you are just guessing.

What is more ethical?

To take the time to refine a program and make it great? Or to just guess?

I would argue that the latter is far more unethical. Not to mention, when you pre-sell your program, you're getting some initial income that validates your idea and the fact that people are willing to pay for it. Plus, it gives you that extra motivational push to get the job done and finish the project!

Much like Kickstarter and much like Pope, this concept has allowed my company to create million-dollar products that *work* consistently.

Remember, the number one thing that will set you apart from the market is how great your product works. If you rely on marketing and sales trickery, that will be a temporary stay of execution. In other words, your business is doomed if you don't focus on making a stellar product.

You cannot rely solely on sales and marketing. No amount of marketing will save a bad product.

If you want to dominate, build a legacy, spread your message, and make an impact on the world, you have to take the time to create something amazing.

That's why when I work with my clients, I not only show them how to sell programs, but I also take the time to show them how to make great programs through our systematic Beta process.

I believe it is more ethical to do so and will result in more sales and more impact in your business.

I don't help people sell crap products. I help people create something tremendous and spread the word to as many people as possible to change their lives.

To me, that is the height of ethics. If you feel differently, perhaps you should put this book down right now. However, if this sounds good to you, then flip to the next chapter.

HOW I MADE $100K IN 30 DAYS: THE BLUEPRINT

The following blueprint is a plan for theoretically making $100,000 in 30 days. The reason I say this is because I made $100,000 in 30 days when I got started. This plan is, to the best of my recollection, exactly how it went down, and the instructions I would give myself if I went back in time.

NOTE: I do not expect you to make 6-figures in 30 days with this plan. I am simply providing you with the blueprint I used to make that happen. Keep in mind, I had all day, every day, to do this. I was not working a nine-to-five job at the time. Still, the opportunity is there no matter how much time you have. Maybe you'll only make $5,000 or $20,000. Perhaps you'll beat me and hit $120,000! Either way, this blueprint is the fast track to selling a course or coaching program even if you have little to no budget.

Day One

Today you'll focus on decision making. Identify something that you are good at that others would want to learn. It could be a minimal skill or a big one. It doesn't matter.

"I will teach [AUDIENCE] how to get [DESIRE]."

Create a Facebook group, mentioning that skill/desire in the name. Use a free graphics program such as Canva to create a cover photo with your smiling mug on it.

Add a link to the group on your personal Facebook profile. Edit your cover photo, bio, and featured sections to include a "Call to Action."

"Want to Learn _____? Join my free Facebook Group [GROUP NAME]."

Now, if anyone comes to your personal profile, they'll see a huge "Call to Action" to join the group immediately.

Next, join several niche groups focused on your target audience. Meaning, people that are discussing the skill you based your Facebook group around.

All of this should get done before lunch. If it takes you longer than lunch, it means you are being too picky with graphics, or you are simply lazy. Deny yourself lunch until it's completed.

Eat.

Now record a quick video welcoming everyone and giving some tips. Post the video in the group. Pin the post/announcement.

Spend the rest of the afternoon interacting in the groups you've joined. Provide value by helping people and answering questions.

Ask open-ended questions and keep comment threads going.

People will see the value, get curious, click your name, see your profile, see the call to action on the cover photo, and join your group. They'll probably send you a friend request as well.

Finish the evening by welcoming each new member personally into your group. There may only be a few, but these are your first steps. Send them a welcome message and get to know them a little bit.

Right before bed, sign up for a Stripe account so you can accept payments and get that out of the way.

It's only day one, but this is what it takes.

Days 2-5

For the next few days, continue providing value in other groups and networking. Make valuable threads in groups and do this until your group has a couple hundred members.

Some groups even have designated days or threads where you can promote your business without violating the group rules. Research the days and times these promo threads get posted in each group, set an alarm on your phone for 10 minutes prior, and be the first one to post an appropriate link when it's time. You mess around on social media all day anyway, so this should be easy.

Day 6

Create a free survey using Google Forms. Call it "Free Training Survey." Ask some questions based around what your audience wants to learn. Ask them what's holding them back and what obstacles are in their way, so you can later utilize their answers to overcome objections.

Create a post in your group, and on your personal page, announcing you will be creating a free eBook or video training on the subject of your group. For instance, if your group is about dog training, then the video training should be about how to train your dog, etc.

Then say, "To make sure the training is awesome, please fill out this survey! I want to cover all your questions on the webinar!"

To keep it at the top of the feed, spend the rest of the day keeping open-ended sub-threads going on this post. That's the secret to engagement. You'll begin getting answers to your form, which will give you everything you need to create sales copy, webinars, and even your offer.

Days 7-8

Continue to promote this survey while writing out bullet points of what you are going to share on this free training.

Begin by identifying the end result everyone wants to achieve.

Refer to their survey answers to find out what obstacle is in the way that they think they need to overcome to get that result. Now, find an alternative path to the end result.

For instance, if people want to learn to be speakers and think they need to network with publicists or agents first, teach them how to land paying speaking gigs even if they don't have an agent or know anyone in the industry.

As long as you can identify the desire and you know you can teach an alternative method (the main obstacle that will get them the goal), they will buy.

Your video training should teach three main things, but you will teach them through storytelling. Sketch out the three things you will teach and come up with a story for each one.

The first story will be an overview of how you discovered the alternative path or the "new way" to achieve their goals. For example, if your audience is made up of actors who believe they must move to LA to network and land roles, find a story from your own life experience that shows them why this belief is false. For example, perhaps you made money as an actor while living in Kansas by solely auditioning online and flying out to gigs!

The second story will cover why this new path will work for them. Even if something is stopping them, they have little control over it. So for the acting offer, they may believe that if they don't have a portfolio, no one will take them seriously. If they can't land roles, how can they have a portfolio to get more gigs?

Tell them the story about how you landed unpaid roles in student films at your local college in exchange for portfolio footage. Now they'll realize they can easily and quickly build a portfolio, leveraging their local college. That's value.

Finally, cover why the new path will work for them even if they feel something is internally wrong with them. For instance, if the actor says, "Great! I can land roles without relocating! I also see I can get a portfolio quickly using student films. But, what if I'm not good at selling myself?"

Find an event from your life to overcome this objection. Share the story of how you thought that as well, but your buddy that introduced you to online auditions told you a secret. The secret? Casting directors do not speak to the actors directly. Agents submit most online auditions, and the agency goes to bat for you if your audition is chosen. All you need is talent, the right look for the role, and availability. Sales are taken care of by the agent.

By the way, I'm making this up for illustrative purposes. I have no idea if this is how online auditions work, or if that's even a real thing.

Get yourself a whiteboard and practice what you will say. By Day 9, this presentation should be ready to go.

Day 9

Announce in your group that the webinar will be held on a specific date. You will be going live in your group. Make sure to include in your post, "Who wants into the webinar?" That way, people will naturally comment, "I do" in the comment box, consistently driving it to the top of the feed.

Host a Facebook Live in your group and give a preview of Secret #1.

Day 10

Do another Facebook Live in the group teaching a preview of Secret #2. Continue to promote the date of the webinar.

Day 11

Repeat what you did for Day 10, but now give a preview of Secret #3.

Day 12

Today is the webinar. Continue hyping it up to make sure everyone is aware of it right until the last minute. Go live and perform your webinar, teaching the three secrets. Once finished, make an offer.

The offer is simple.

Announce that you plan to launch an online course covering in detail what you shared on the webinar.

Then, do the Beta Pitch:

"I'm going to make a special one-time offer right here, right now. If you get in now, you'll not only get the course for half price, but you'll also get to take part in a group coaching session. I will personally teach it to you and answer all of your questions live during the training. I'll make SURE you understand everything!"

Since people may not know or trust you yet, mention that you are going to offer something better than a refund. You'll charge them $1 today, and they won't get charged the full price until 48 hours after the live coaching session. That way, they can try it before they buy it.

If they don't like it, they can send you an email within 48 hours after the training and request to cancel. Cancel the charge, and they'll never even have to pay for it.

Then make a secondary offer. If they are 100% in and don't care about the refund guarantee, they can pay in full right now for an extra discount.

Let's say you charge $300 and 10 people take the offer. You now have $3,000 soon to be in your pocket.

If you don't sell a single copy, you know that there's something fundamentally wrong with the offer. You can now put a halt to this right away before wasting too much time.

If you had spent the entire time creating a program, you would've wasted all that time once you discovered no one wanted it. By identifying this potential problem early, you now have time to fix it.

Days 13-15

The coaching session is in a few days. Spend those few days coming up with very quick and ugly bullet point slides to present to your students. Don't spend time on making it look nice; what's most important is the content.

Day 16

Now it's time for a group coaching session. I prefer Zoom webinars to host the sessions, but you can use whatever you like; just make sure there is a Q&A box.

Begin teaching each lesson doing the best you can to make what you are teaching clear. Then at the end of the lesson, ask for questions. Answer each question thoroughly and completely.

If you feel that people don't understand what you are teaching, mark that lesson as needing revision. Or re-explain on the spot, and write down the time in the video when it happened. You can edit out the bad explanation later and keep the good one.

If you need to completely redo any lesson, offer it 100% for free on a different day. Revise your work to make sure they love it.

Complete the group coaching session and ask for feedback.

If feedback is overwhelmingly positive, bring them on camera and ask for an on-the-spot testimonial. They will be super hyped, so the testimonial will be good. Now you have social proof for use in your marketing, and it's only been two weeks.

Days 17-18

You should now have a several hour video file from your group coaching day. Over the next two days, mark out where lessons should begin and end. Notate any mistakes to get cut.

When the day comes for everyone to get charged, make sure all the charges go through. If anyone wants to cancel, cancel their charge and get some feedback from them.

If you do everything correctly, you should get little to no cancellation requests. I only received one the last time I did this, and it was only because the guy didn't have any money. If you made 10 initial sales and got only one or two cancellations, you should have at least $2,300 in your pocket. However, the first time I did it, I had close to $4,000.

Before bed, create an account on Fiverr or Upwork and hire someone to edit the lessons. Send them the "time-based edits" document you made, and let them work. That should cost no more than $500. Now you have at least $1,800 left.

Continue to promote your group.

Day 19

Use the questions, pain points, and feedback from the coaching session to create a free PDF report offering some tips and value. Also, start working on what you will say on your next live webinar. You should be refining it from what you learned from selling your Beta offer.

Once you get the videos back from the editor, load them into a membership portal. Upload the "end of the coaching session testimonials" to YouTube or other video hosting platform.

Days 20-24

Now that you have money in your pocket, run your first Facebook ad (or YouTube ad) offering to give away a free cheat sheet. Funnel prospects into your Facebook group by inviting them on the confirmation page and welcome email. Spend about $1,000 on ads for the cheat sheet. This should get you several hundred prospects on your email list and in your group over the next week.

Host live videos and hype up the new webinar in your group over the next several days. These videos will direct them to a registration page for a new live webinar. This webinar will be more refined and have a complete offer stack with an order page at the end.

Day 25

Broadcast the webinar and make the offer. After pitching your product, there is a super ninja trick I discovered that increases sales. It's just something I tried once and it worked fantastically. Tell them if they want to get into the private group, they need to post in your free group and say, "Hey [YOUR NAME], I just bought the program. Please add me to the student group."

Then screen share the live feed of the group during the offer pitch and actually show the "I just bought" posts live! This will cause extreme mob mentality and a buying spree.

This is how I made $48,000, my very first webinar, and $52,000 on my encore a week later. I created a mob mentality, and I barely had a list.

Days 26-28

Schedule an encore webinar and promote the heck out of it for the next several days. Keep the cheat sheet ad running. More money will be coming in, so you can spend more on ads.

Day 29

It's possible to pull $30,000 to $50,000 out of this initial webinar and another $30,000 to $50,000 a week later with an encore.

This brings you close to a 6-figure month starting from nothing.

I know this is possible because this is what I did when I hit $100,000 in my first month.

Even if you only generate 1/5 of that, you still will have made around $20,000. If you don't, it simply just means you need help. The problem could be your offer, your webinar, etc. It's normal to need help. If everyone could do this on the first try without help, the entire world would be millionaires.

Day 30

Relax. Then start refining your program immediately. Make it the best possible product out there because THAT is what it will take to scale.

Final Thoughts

If there is an audience willing to learn something for free, there will always be some willing to pay for more. You only need 1% of your audience to buy to become a millionaire and change the world at the same time.

THE WHITEBOARD
WEBINAR

In this chapter, I will share a secret that revolutionized my business. It's called "The Whiteboard Webinar."

Now, before I share this, let's back up a bit so I can give you a little background.

There is one method of selling that has been responsible for 99% of my income, and that is a webinar.

Now, you may hear some disgruntled noise in the market that webinars don't work anymore, or maybe you're entirely unfamiliar with what webinars are.

Webinars are just online presentations. The webinar format has been around for thousands of years!

The format is simple. You give a presentation, teach something of value, and then at the end, ask those viewers to buy an offer that allows them to execute on the knowledge they just gained.

Ever been in a Sam's Club or Costco? Have you seen those people behind the booths that offer a free gift if you watch a presentation? They're basically doing in-person webinars!

For instance, let's say you attend a presentation on how to save money on your electric. The presenter shows you that you're spending way too much with your power company, and you could save so much more with solar panels!

So you think, "Wow, I would save so much money with solar panels, but I just can't afford them."

Then all of a sudden, before that thought can even complete in your mind, the person behind the booth says, "Here's how anyone can afford solar panels!"

They then proceed to tell you about tax credits, financing, and all kinds of things that overcome your objections of why you can't have what you want.

This entire presentation is a webinar. The only difference is that we call them sales presentations offline and call them webinars online.

This method is precisely how we sell millions of dollars in high-ticket products online.

If properly executed, a webinar can scale your company to 7- or 8- figures in a very short time. But it must be done "properly."

When I launched my first webinar, I was just winging it. I made zero sales. Then I went out and bought books, coaching, and learned everything I could to learn more about this process.

I invested time and money into learning this craft.

My next webinar? I generated $48,000 in two hours. Fast forward to today, and I've made over $10 million with just two properly crafted webinars.

Now that you know how well webinars work, let me tell you how most people approach them and why it's a mistake.

Typically, a webinar contains tons of slides, graphics, illustrations, perhaps a countdown timer, and all kinds of little nifty bells and whistles to squeeze the maximum amount of sales out of your presentation.

However, people often use these as a crutch and spend weeks or even months building these out. They create what they would consider their masterpiece, then launch the webinar, and no one buys.

I've only made this mistake once, and I will never make it again.

Would you like to know how to find out if that webinar you're planning on creating will actually work? Would you like to know within 30 minutes, instead of weeks or months?

Let me tell you a little story about one of the highest converting webinars I've ever made.

A couple of friends of mine, Todd Snively and Chris Keef, came over to my house to talk business. They were interested in doing a joint venture at the time. This means I would create a product, sell it to their existing list, and we would split the profits. The plan was to meet, discuss our ideas, and then plan a date to launch.

However, we had a few drinks that day, and I wanted to try something crazy.

I said, "Why are we talking about doing a JV? Why don't we just do one right now?"

Todd and Chris looked at me sort of confused and said, "What do you mean?"

I said, "Tell me about your audience and their biggest struggle. I'll come up with a product to solve the problem. We'll jump on a Facebook Live in 20 minutes, and I'll sell it to them."

Confused, they asked me, "Well, you haven't created the product yet?"

I said, "Yeah, so we're going to give them a 50% discount, I'll film it next week and send an email out the following week so they can enjoy the offer and get in on this nice little pre-sale."

Todd and Chris thought this was a stellar idea. All three of us are very busy people, so this made a ton of sense. If no one bought, then we don't have to do any work! If they do buy, then we do the work we already got paid for, and their customers enjoy a significant discount for getting in early. Everyone wins.

They agreed to move forward. So after hearing the problems their audience had, I knew right away what I could teach to solve them. I didn't have all the details fleshed out yet, but that didn't matter—more on that in a moment.

So they went into their Facebook group, announced they were going to be doing a special impromptu training, and told everyone to hop on the live in 20 minutes. I quickly scribbled down what the offer was and what I was going to say on the live.

Chris held his phone up; it was just a little iPhone, which back then was nothing more than a crappy iPhone 7. I went live, shared a few stories on a whiteboard on how to overcome their problems and then made the offer. This lasted about 25 minutes. Once we ended the live, I checked sales.

We made $25,000! In 25 minutes. That's about $1,000 per minute! I could not believe my eyes!

I then filmed the product over the next couple of weeks and sent it to those who'd purchased.

I had a huge epiphany that week. I learned you don't need bells and whistles, false scarcity, timers, chat windows, fancy slides, or graphics to make money with a presentation.

If your offer makes sense to your audience, they will buy it. If it doesn't, no amount of fancy graphics or advanced webinar software will save you.

Will those things help? Sure they will, but they will not fix something that will never sell. They will not take an offer that no one wants and make them want the offer. They will simply enhance and squeeze a few extra sales out of an offer that people already want.

So, the first step is to make sure that people actually want your offer. That is why I absolutely love the whiteboard webinar method.

With this method, you're able to, with little to no preparation, craft a message, and deliver it. You strip yourself of all those fancy tools and see if it sells in its rawest form. If it sells raw, it can scale.

If you can nail the message and the offer with nothing more than an iPhone and a whiteboard, you now have a seed that will surely grow into a million-dollar business.

Plus, you now have validation that it's okay to take the next couple of weeks and build out a fancy webinar with fancy emails and fancy automation.

At the end of the day, if you can't get past the whiteboard webinar and make a few sales, you have absolutely no business building out a huge email campaign, creating hundreds of slides, or building a complicated webinar funnel.

I remember one of my clients, Arnie, came to me and was struggling with an offer. He tried so many times to build out a full webinar, and it just didn't work. So I told him about this white-board webinar method, and he decided to give it a go.

However, things went terribly wrong. Arnie went live, and no one could see the whiteboard! He had set up too many lights, and the board was completely white and, therefore, illegible on camera!

At the last minute, he had to put down his marker, sit down in front of the computer and just talk to the camera. So with no white-board, he shared his message and his offer.

He made $16,000 that day.

Today, he has $100,000 months.

What is the moral of this story? It's simple. Break something down, stripping it down to its most raw and simple form. If it still works, it's a winner. However, if it takes complicated bells and whistles just to make a sale, it will fall apart at scale.

"Our life is frittered away by detail ... simplify, simplify."

— Henry David Thoreau

The Power of Polarity

"If you're always trying to be normal, you will never know how amazing you can be."

— *Maya Angelou*

My brand began kicking off during the 2016 election when I noticed that Donald Trump was doing all this crazy stuff, saying the craziest things. And he ends up getting elected as the President of the United States!

And I remember noticing and paying attention to what was actually happening. I noticed a few very important things. He would intentionally say stuff just to get in the headlines.

He reached the media outlets that were opposing him (who thought they were hurting him), but they were actually helping him reach more of the people that resonated with him.

He had 10 times more free media exposure than all of his opponents combined.

And it was at that moment I realized that if you make enough noise, all eyes will be on you. Make sure you're selling something.

I also realized that if I wanted to stand out, I had to make a splash.

So I went in this popular Facebook group that at the time was all about being yourself in your business.

I posted a picture of me naked on the couch with nothing but a little smiley face as a cover-up, and I said:

"Who wants to learn marketing from this guy?"

And it blew up!

There were hundreds and hundreds of comments.

It was the first time I decided to put myself out there.

Prior to that, I had been boring and professional—what I thought other people wanted me to be.

It was the first time I decided to take a chance and just be myself. (My father was a shock jock in the 80s, if that gives you any clue to my sense of humor.)

When I did, it blew up so much that people started friend-requesting me, joining my Facebook group, and following me.

It was the initial thing that made people actually start becoming fans. It was different, and I was unapologetic about it.

I basically modeled not what Donald Trump was doing exactly, but the idea of leverage, and I applied it to my marketing efforts.

I noticed that every time he did something that would have ruined the career of any other politician, (that would make any other politician, historically, resign), all he did was shrug it off.

Everybody was upset about it, but because he didn't engage and he didn't apologize and he didn't play into it, everybody forgot about it and they were talking about something else a week later.

That's when I realized that, even though they say it takes a lifetime to build a reputation and only a few minutes to destroy it, I don't believe that is true. I believe that you can say something and make a mistake and as long as you don't feed into it, when people call you out on it, eventually they'll forget.

Countless times in my marketing career, I would try to apply an advertising angle or something that ended up not working out or ended up offending a lot of people—not my intention to offend them, but it just did.

Basically, I said the wrong thing. And instead of apologizing and making a big deal about it, I just stayed quiet and eventually everybody forgot about it.

I would then post a picture of me and my son or a family trip, and I realized, nobody cares anymore. They're like, "Oh, what a sweet baby!"

Public opinion is easily turned around. It moves back and forth, back and forth.

The reason I'm telling you this is because if you are afraid of saying the wrong thing, you will end up saying nothing.

Don't put so much pressure on yourself to always say the right thing. Now, I'm not telling you to post naked pictures of yourself online, but put yourself out there. You *will* say the wrong thing. And as long as you don't make a big deal about it and you don't acknowledge all the people that disagree with you, and you just keep moving forward, they'll forget, and eventually they could become fans.

Here's a little trick in your marketing when it comes to polarity.

Imagine you're sitting at a bar and you have two people on either side of you. The person to your left is your ideal customer; the person to your right is someone who would never, ever buy from you.

Say something to start a fight.

If you say something that gets them to argue, they will do the promoting for you.

For instance, I had a program that taught people how to start an advertising agency, and I knew because it was geared toward beginners that seasoned marketers (older, seasoned marketers—people that may have taken big certifications, spent money on email software certifications, etc.), would never buy this program, but new people to the industry would.

So I thought, "What can I say that will offend the people that wouldn't buy so that they make enough noise to capture the attention of the people that would buy."

And so I said, "Listen, the truth is there's a new way to advertise. And if you do it, you can outperform almost all of the seasoned and experienced marketers and get just as good results as they do—do not believe their lies."

"You don't need to attend a $10,000 marketing certification seminar to get results for a local business. You can get by with just a couple of weeks' worth of training. And if you do it this way, you can get just as good results as the seasoned marketers—and that's going to piss them off."

And when I said that, a ton of seasoned marketers started saying, "Oh, screw Dan Henry."

But alas, something amazing happened. New marketers would see these posts and say, "Well, why? What did he do that was so bad?"

The seasoned marketers would argue, "Oh, he's saying that newbies can make just as much money as us and get just as good results." And when they do that, and they comment, and they tag, a lot of those people who would resonate with that message end up listening and buying my stuff.

In fact, I regularly survey my customers and ask where they initially heard of me. Many say it was from someone else bad-mouthing me. A surprising number, in fact. Think about how much more bang for your buck you could get with your advertising budget if you introduced some polarity into your message.

And so that is one way you can use polarity in your marketing.

Always say something or try to say something that really resonates with your target customer but would also offend your non-target customer so that they create enough noise to help you make a splash.

"Peace does not mean an absence of conflict, because opposition, polarity and conflict are natural and universal laws."

— Bryant McGill

SCALING YOUR

How We Scaled
to 8-Figures

If I had to describe my journey to that first $100,000 in one word, it would be a "Launch."

Most people call it: "The Live Launch."

It's where you manually build hype, launch a product, and then you make a bunch of money all at once.

However, that's not how I scaled 8-figures. If I would've kept doing that, I would not be anywhere near the growth I am currently.

"But wait, you made $100,000 in 30 days, Dan! You're telling me that's not the best way?"

Yes, that's what I'm telling you. I would have been just as shocked if someone said that to me. Sure, it was the best way to test, the best way to get started, but terrible for scale. But let me tell you precisely what happened that led me to this discovery.

After I had made that initial $100,000 doing a live launch, I was exhausted. It was a lot of pressure in planning, and I was spent.

So I planned to take a 30-day break, casually work on the materials for the new launch, and then do it again. If I made $100,000 every time I did it, that would be a pretty good income!

However, it's not 8-figures. Little did I know that was even possible.

So during this break, I did not like the idea of making no money at all. Sure, I had $100,000 in the bank, but I still wanted some income between breaks.

I decided to take the replay of my webinar and put it on a page where people could watch it instantly.

My idea was to run ads to it and make some sales here and there until the next big launch.

This was great! Because once you create paid advertisements on social media platforms, they don't need much maintenance. Unlike organic marketing, where you are posting every single day on various platforms.

So that's what I did, and I wasn't expecting much. But when that first sale came in while I was sleeping, it felt even more amazing than making all that money in one day. It was only one sale, but something about making money without having to be present was fascinating to me.

But then another sale came in, and another, and another. At the end of the 30-day break, I was shocked to see that we had generated $150,000 in sales. That's $50,000 more than when I did the live launch! And I didn't have to lift a finger past setting up the video and ads.

This brought me to a whole new high, and it was at that moment I had an epiphany.

I realized that as amazing as it is to grind yourself to the bone and do a live promotion, as much money as that brings, automating your sales brings more.

"Slow and steady wins the race," as the old adage says.

Did you know a small leak in your faucet that drips for just one day outputs five gallons of water?

Sales trickling in all day every day will almost always beat a flood gate of sales here and there.

Once I realized that the key to growing was by automating sales and not doing live promotions, I decided to become a master of that method.

Not to mention, this fits my lifestyle much more. While it may not be fully 100% passive income, it's 1,000 times more passive than doing any live promotion.

That's not to say I don't still do live promotions here and there. Usually, it's when I'm testing out a new product or a new version of a product.

Remember that initial webinar that made $150,000 automated

during its first month?

It was a crude prototype that eventually became a well-oiled machine.

Over the next couple of years, I refined and mastered the art of that automated process. So much so, that we were able to hit our first million-dollar month revenue in February 2019 with only two automated webinars.

That's right, a million dollars in one month with only two products.

There's absolutely no way I could do those types of numbers day in and day out running around dancing on social media.

And even if I could, I wouldn't want to. I didn't get into this business to work myself to death. I got in it to help people and enjoy life.

At this point, you're probably wondering how this automated sales system works.

It has two main components: the system and the script. The script is what you say on the webinar and the system is how we deliver that webinar to our prospect.

I'm going to give you the basic strategy behind it right now, but I will not be sharing tactics. Why? Because by the time you read this book, I will probably have refined it further and tweaked some things to make it even more profitable.

That's why I share strategy in books, which are more permanent, and I share tactics online in the form of video training, which can be easily updated.

If you'd like to learn what's currently working right now, you can watch an overview of our automated sales system by visiting **DigitalMillionaireSecrets.com/system**.

However, the strategy has not changed, nor do I see it ever changing.

So let me break down the underlying strategy behind this automated sales system, or as I prefer to call it, an "On-Demand Webinar."

A potential prospect that has a problem will see an advertisement online. This could be Facebook, Instagram, YouTube. It could even be on a piece of direct mail.

The advertisement offers a short training that will help them solve their problem or at least part of it.

They click the advertisement and go to a page where they can enter their name and email to access the free video.

We refer to this usually as a webinar. But we have other types of videos, such as case studies, to achieve similar results.

Once they enter their information, they can watch the video. We share a ton of value in this video and show them how we can solve their problem.

We then make an offer where they can pay for a premium training.

If they are convinced that this product will solve their problem, they buy. If not, then they get multiple follow-up emails and marketing to help get them off the fence.

Speaking of "The Fence," in the next chapter, I will reveal more details on how we follow up with prospects that are still thinking of buying, but have not yet committed.

But for now, the main point I want to make to you is simple. While we have tried lots of things on our road to 8-figures, this system has been responsible for the majority of sales.

Sure, we've used other methods that have fantastic results, and we share those methods with our clients.

But if you could only allow me one strategy to market my business, it would be hands-down an On-Demand Webinar.

Once you master the art of what to say in your webinar, you have something that can print money on demand.

I can thank Russell Brunson for introducing me to webinars and more importantly, what to say on them. After reading several books from Russell, I continued my education and learned from a variety of entrepreneurs that had crushed it with webinars.

Eventually, I created and tweaked my own concoction into what is now our low-ticket and high-ticket webinar frameworks.

Perhaps it's the artist in me, but I've always been a big believer in refinement. Art is truly never finished.

When you sell 8-figures with a webinar, you tend to figure out what works, what doesn't, and what works better pretty rapidly.

We are still tweaking it to this day, which brought me to the decision I had to make while writing this book.

To share our Webinar script here or not?

On the one hand, I could lay it all out for you here, but what bothered me about that is the fact that books are so permanent.

If we develop new tactics, then the book becomes outdated.

So I decided to go for a second option. As a bonus for buying this book, you will get a free training on the current webinar script and framework that we use.

All you have to do is go to **DigitalMillionaireSecrets.com/script.**

If we make any major breakthroughs, we will update that video, so you'll always have access to the most up-to-date tactics.

Tactics change; strategy doesn't.

This book is about strategy, and the bonuses you get with it are about tactics.

I wanted to over-deliver with this book, which is why I'm giving you far more than just the book. So if you want to check out the script we currently use, head over to that link.

In the following chapter, I'm going to show you what we do when a prospect doesn't say yes right away on the webinar. I will also show you how we've converted millions of dollars in sales from prospects that just weren't sure yet.

"Not following up with your prospects is the same as filling up your bathtub without first putting the stopper in the drain."

— Michelle Moore

THE FENCE METHOD

In the 1930s, the film industry made a startling discovery.

The studios found that a certain amount of advertising was necessary to convince people to see their movies.

They discovered that people needed to see an advertisement at least seven times before they decided to buy a movie ticket.

This discovery bled over into other industries and proved to be almost universally applicable.

Regardless of the product, advertisers found prospects needed to see a message seven times before they decided to buy.

Today, this is known as "The Rule of Seven."

Considering this rule was discovered back in the 1930s, before we entered the digital age, we can assume that the average person had a much longer attention span when this rule was discovered.

Today, we're constantly bombarded with messages. Common sense should tell us that people need to see our messages even more than seven times before they decide to buy.

That's why now, more than ever, following up with your prospects is extremely important.

But how does this look for the webinar model?

When your prospects go into your webinar, they come out in one of three possible scenarios.

They either say "YES" and buy it immediately...

They say "ABSOLUTELY NOT" and never buy...

Or they say "MAYBE."

"Maybe" is also known as "On The Fence."

Why do we call it this?

Imagine your prospects are physically standing on top of a fence.

They are teetering on a thin rail and can easily fall to either the YES side or the NO side at any time.

Now, I am not a data scientist, but based on my experience and looking at our data, I can estimate about 2% of people say "YES" immediately, 30% say "ABSOLUTELY NOT," and 68% are "MAYBE" or "On The Fence."

If you were to completely ignore that 68%, you would basically be staring at a pile of money on the table in front of you, simply choosing not to pick it up.

That said, once the prospect leaves the webinar and does not buy, we continuously send them new content designed to knock them to the "YES" side of the fence.

Tactically, this could be in the form of retargeting ads, emails, videos, podcast episodes, etc.

Strategically, they all have the same goal in mind. To knock the prospect off the fence and get them to buy.

Most of the time, it is much more than seven pieces of content. We keep chucking stuff at them until eventually they fall and become a customer.

The content is designed to overcome any objections that a potential prospect may have. Giving them more information, typically, the type of information they may need to make a decision.

However, if you are not sending the right content, you could easily knock the prospect on the NO side. I know this because when I first started, instead of knocking them onto the YES side, I accidentally pushed them onto the NO side.

Early in my career, I thought to follow up meant to send the prospect sales pitch after sales pitch continuously. However, this did not work out. It only made customers angry.

Our webinar was doing very well, but our follow up was not so hot.

One day, frustrated, I decided to call a customer on the phone randomly.

I said, "Hey, this is Dan Henry. You recently signed up for my webinar, and I have a question for you. We are trying to improve our marketing. If you can answer this question, I'll give you the product for free. Why didn't you buy?"

My goal was to find out how I could fix our follow-up.

It worked better than expected. This person listed off over a dozen reasons why they didn't buy!

The funny thing was, none of the reasons were actual problems with the product. I simply hadn't covered that concern in my webinar, covered it well enough, or they just didn't see that part of the webinar.

After this experience, I was extremely excited because I instantly knew how to (at a very minimum), 10X my sales.

All I needed to do was call a bunch of customers, figure out what all the objections were, and start creating emails and videos that covered each one!

However, I also realized that I would be on the phone for weeks if I tried to do that with a phone call each time.

So I created a little questionnaire that asked some specific questions as to why they didn't buy.

I emailed it to everybody that watched my webinar but didn't buy, and I got hundreds of responses back!

Do you know what the funny thing was? Even though we had hundreds of responses, the objections were mostly the same.

I categorized them all by the number of times they appeared and found that there were only about 15 to 20 objections. Everyone was essentially saying the same thing!

So I started making videos covering each one of these things and sending them out email by email, asking people to watch the video.

I didn't try to sell people. I simply gave them the information they needed to alleviate their concerns.

For instance, one of the objections to our Sold Out Courses program was:

"I have yet to create my course, and I'm still not confident the program will get my students results. So until I'm confident in my product and I finish creating it, I can't buy your program!"

Now, this almost made me blow a gasket. A huge chunk of our program teaches you how to build the product correctly, from the beginning (so it scales). It also shows you how to make sure your students get results.

We have systems and worksheets designed to poll your students and help you quickly make adjustments to your program that get them better and better results.

In fact, one of the core elements of the sales strategy we teach our clients is that a great product is easy to sell. A bad product is hard to sell. So let's first focus on making sure your product is great.

It could have been that I may not have explained that particular aspect of our program well enough in our webinar. Even if I did, chances are some people may not have been paying attention during that part. Maybe it just wasn't enough to overcome that concern at the time.

So I created three videos.

One was a case study on a student who was able to redesign his program that students hated, into one that his people loved. He went from a few grand per month to $20,000 per month just by making his program better.

The next email was an overview of one of the first things you have to do to make a great program. At the end of teaching the outline, I held nothing back. I asked if they would like more help implementing it. I then encouraged them to consider our product.

The third email was me getting on a soapbox, talking about how there are far too many bad products currently in the market. Instead of trying to focus on sleazy sales tactics, we should instead try to make great products. If you join our program, that's what we help you do.

All three of these videos had value instead of just a blatant sales pitch.

Once we sent these emails out, the sales started pouring in. So I started making more videos and more videos and more videos. Sales went up, up, and you guessed it, up!

We took it a step further. Every year, I would adjust the script and make sure to cover these concerns more efficiently on the actual webinar.

As a result, both the initial webinar, as well as the follow-up, continuously got better and better!

So, naturally, I started teaching this method to my clients.

One of our clients, Steven, was quite successful with his webinar when he joined my mastermind.

He was generating approximately $25,000 a month with his webinar and educational program. But once I taught him the "Didn't Buy Survey," he was able to double his conversion rate for his webinar.

We doubled his sales by teaching him just that one thing.

After about six months in the program, we kept showing Steven more and more ways to scale his education business. He was eventually able to break $100,000 per month.

He made one of the funniest testimonial videos I've ever received. In it, he said something to the effect of, "I'm not supposed to do these numbers. I'm not that smart. If an idiot like me can do this, that means Dan's program is pretty damn good."

When I told Steven I was going to include this method in this book, he almost got mad at me.

He was wondering why I would share such an effective tactic in a book that sells for a few dollars.

The way I look at it, if I never share this stuff, I'll probably stop innovating.

If I give some of my best stuff away for free, it will force me to innovate and become even better.

Again, I'm addicted to refinement.

Nelson Mandela said, "The greatest glory in living lies not in never falling, but in rising every time we fall."

I've always loved this quote, which inspired a quote of my own.

Dan Henry says, "Picking yourself up is not enough; you must learn how to fall with grace."

See, when a process fails, most people think of it as a failure. I like to view it as the data needed for success.

There is an art to failure, and it's the fastest way to success.

THE GOLDFISH RULE

"On average, five times as many people read the headline as read the body copy. When you have written your headline, you have spent eighty cents out of your dollar."

— *David Ogilvy*

H ave you ever tried to entertain a goldfish?

Think about it. What would you say to a goldfish as it darts around its tank, to get its attention? Could you?

If you can, then you will likely be pretty good at advertising. If not, advertising will be a massive issue for you.

In 1970, the average attention span of an American was 12 minutes.

Today, the average attention span is under nine seconds. That is less than a goldfish.[9]

If you could ask me for one tip when it comes to advertising for your product, it would be what I like to call, "The Goldfish Rule."

Yes, this one is mine, so make sure you quote me if you share it!

The Goldfish Rule states, "In any advertisement, identify what's in it for the prospect in nine seconds or less."

Most people make this grave mistake when starting. This applies to any paid ad, social media post, email, or any messaging that's sent to your prospect.

How many times have you seen an advertisement that starts with a long story? Often, you have to read through Edgar-Allan-Poe-style writing before they get to the point!

People do not have that much time today, nor are they willing to give you that time. You must earn it.

Think of all of the distractions in the world today. We have such a short attention span that we have even created social media platforms based on making videos that are 15 seconds or less. New platforms have come out with even shorter time frames.

How do you stand out in such a world? An entire population is darting their eyes around like a goldfish in a tank.

You simply follow "The Goldfish Rule."

I wish I had some fancy story to tell you about how I discovered this. I don't. It's something I learned from spending millions of dollars on advertising.

Within the first nine seconds, you must tell them what they are going to get out of continuing to read or listen. If you can do it in less than nine seconds, even better.

Once you have successfully done this, you will have earned the right for a little bit more of their time. If the rest of your advertisement is good, then you may earn the right to get more from them, such as contact information or even a sale.

Most people attempt to do this using what's called a "Pattern Interrupt."

It's called a "Pattern Interrupt" because it interrupts the existing pattern in your brain and causes you to pay attention. It's used in almost all industries.

Speakers will often raise their voice to wake the audience up and get them to pay attention. Print advertisements will often use a pretty girl to capture the readers' attention, etc.

In online marketing, most people try to say something outrageous at the very beginning of the ad.

That is not enough.

We don't just want to grab anyone's attention. We want to grab the attention of those who need our product.

That's why we use what I like to call an "Identifying Pattern Interrupt."

Let's take a look at three approaches.

No Pattern Interrupt, Pattern Interrupt, and Identifying Pattern Interrupt.

Let's say you are trying to sell a speaking course.

Let's start with No Pattern Interrupt. Most advertisements or email copy would start out something like this:

> *There I was. Nervously fidgeting with the application I just sent through. You see it was 5 a.m. and I just couldn't sleep.*
>
> *I really wanted to land this gig, but I also knew the other speakers had more experience than me.*

Most people think this is decent copy. But most people don't know what they're doing. So that makes sense.

This might sound like a great story. But, if you are a speaker looking to grow your speaking business, you wouldn't be aware this advertisement applies to you. You wouldn't know until you read the end of the second paragraph. By that time, many have already moved on.

Thinking it's different if it's in an email? Why? Because they have already signed up for your list? It's not. Most people don't remember signing up on an email list. They need a constant reminder of why they're reading an email from your company.

Don't believe me? Take a look at every email you've ever sent to your list. You'll find that every single one has spam complaints.

Maybe it's only one or two, but they are still there. It's because people don't remember.

So now we try to use a Pattern Interrupt to earn their attention.

Let's try this again with a pattern interrupt:

> *Mr. Smith, you have cancer.*
>
> *Thankfully, I woke up from the nightmare I just had. I didn't have cancer, but I did have a nightmare about it. Likely because I had been so nervous all night, any sleep I got was plagued by bad dreams.*
>
> *After sipping my third cup of coffee, I nervously fidgeted with the application I just sent through.*
>
> *I really wanted to land this gig, but I also knew the other speakers had more experience than me.*

Now, as shocking and attention-grabbing as that first sentence is, what does a nightmare about having cancer have to do with speaking?

Not a darn thing.

Again, this is copy from someone who thinks they know what they are doing, but they simply do not.

How do I know this? Because this is the type of copy I wrote for years early in my career.

It wasn't until I spent millions of dollars on advertising that I began to see the upper echelon of what works.

I don't think I could have learned that anywhere unless I was speaking with someone who also had spent millions of dollars on advertising.

Those people are few and far between.

So let's take a look at what this would look like if we used an Identifying Pattern Interrupt:

> *This was the third time I had to wipe the vomit off of a speaking application. You see, I had applied for every single conference that entire year, hoping to land my first paid speaking gig.*
>
> *I was scared my lunch would literally come up and onto the application before I could even get to the part where they rejected me.*
>
> *My friends always told me I was freaking out over nothing, yet every time, it always ended the same. 'I'm sorry, it's going to be a no.'*
>
> *I still chuckle back at this time in my life, because last year I spoke at 24 paid speaking events.*
>
> *So what changed?*

If you notice, right from the very beginning, if you are a speaker, it is blatantly apparent this applies to you.

Not to mention, it changed the dynamic of the rest of the copy. Everything is a constant reminder that in no uncertain terms, "this applies to you."

If someone doesn't think something applies to them, they will not gift you their time in order to even see if it does apply to them.

Meaning, you have to be able to create advertisements and marketing that can get a goldfish to buy.

If you try to be artistic or feel that being so blatant in the beginning is beneath you, well, then all I can say is, enjoy your nine-to-five.

In today's day and age, you must get to the point.

So right now, go back and look at every advertisement or email you've ever written.

Does the first sentence clearly, beyond a shadow of a doubt, capture attention? Does it only capture the attention of someone that is your ideal prospect?

Back in the old days, there was no such thing as "conversion optimization."

If you put an advertisement on a billboard, the billboard would not recognize which people driving down the road end up buying your product. The billboard would not adjust traffic so that people who were more likely to buy would see your advertisement, and people less likely to buy wouldn't.

In today's digital age, almost every advertising platform has some sort of conversion optimization.

Meaning, the more people that engage with your advertisement, the more that platform will show your advertisement to similar people.

So if you're just saying something to capture anyone's attention, then that's what you will get more of: anyone.

But if you say something that would only capture the attention of your intended prospect, then guess what happens? More people will see your advertisement that are more likely to buy.

We can talk all day about pressing buttons in any given ads dashboard, tagging people in email software, etc.

But at the end of the day, none of that matters without great messaging.

Meaning, what you *say* in your advertisements.

It's your ability to capture your prospects' attention and get them to take the next step on their way to becoming a part of your customer base.

If you'd like to see a few examples of how I have implemented The Goldfish Method in my own advertisements, you can visit **DigitalMillionaireSecrets.com/goldfish**.

"The real fact of the matter is that nobody reads ads. People read what interests them, and sometimes it's an ad."

— Howard Luck Gossage

How We Tripled Profits with High-Ticket Offers

For the first $8 million in revenue, I didn't change a thing. I advertised a free training, sent people to my webinar, and they bought from an order page.

"I never spoke to a soul, and I loved how passive the income was."

That's what I would tell you if I was just trying to sell you and I had no transparency or ethics.

The actual reality of this business is that there are far more things involved than sitting back on a beach with a laptop while the money rolls in.

With thousands of customers, being at that level of scale, my business was anything but passive.

In the beginning, from zero to $1 million, it was actually pretty passive. I didn't need to spend much time managing it. But once I scaled past that, things got a bit more complicated.

At a lower scale, I only had to deal with certain things here and there. But with that many customers and transactions, I ended up having to hire people to help out.

For instance, I didn't get a single refund request for my first six months in business. If someone had a problem, they would usually message me on Facebook, and I would respond. They were happy. (Now I don't even look at my inbox; my team does.)

But when a dozen customers turned into 100, 100 turned into 1,000, and 1,000 turned into 10,000, there was no way I could respond to every single person on my own.

The funny thing was, 99% of the time, the customer complaint was something simple. Usually, it was something like they didn't get their username and password in their email. Or their receipt went to spam. Or their computer crashed in the middle of buying.

Most of these issues would only take a five-minute conversation to resolve, and the customer was happy. However, when you add up hundreds of five-minute blocks, now you have a real time-consumer on your hands.

In fact, I was so busy that I really couldn't respond to anyone at all. I had to hire customer service representatives to talk to our customers.

While our refund rate had been low, due to the sheer amount of transactions, we had to have a dedicated team to deal with them.

That cost money.

Not to mention, we started getting fraudulent charges. People began using stolen credit cards to buy our products.

Eventually, I had to hire someone to handle disputes and charge-backs.

That cost money.

I remember when one of my early programs got pirated. Someone uploaded it onto a website that cost $50 to access thousands of courses.

So now a new department came into play, the piracy department.

I had someone that would reach out to these websites, negotiate with them, file DMCA (Digital Millennium Copyright Act) complaints, and eventually get the page taken down.

This, as well, cost more time and more money.

That was until I met Alex Hormozi.

At the time, we were both in Russell Brunson's Mastermind. We were standing in line waiting to receive awards for making a million dollars at Russell's annual marketing conference, Funnel Hacking Live.

Alex sells a program that helps gym owners efficiently run their businesses and increase their membership numbers. At the time, he was making about $2 million per month with that program.

But here is where it gets quite interesting.

We started chatting, and I asked him about advertising.

He then said the strangest thing I've ever heard in my life.

"I suck at advertising. But it doesn't matter, because my lowest price program is $16,000."

I stood there for a moment about to speak. Stopped, opened my mouth again. Stopped.

He could tell I was at a loss for words. He interjected, "Dan, when you sell high-ticket, it really doesn't matter what your advertising costs are, you always make money."

Most people don't realize this, but when you only spend a couple of thousand dollars per month on advertising, getting a 10X return is pretty standard.

When you're spending several thousand dollars per month on ads, doubling your money is considered amazing.

That's because as you scale, advertising costs go up, and margins go down.

Not to mention, the fact that your internal expenses go up because you have more customers to manage.

At this time, I had built a reputation that some would argue positioned me as one of the best in the world at online advertising.

Whether that is true or not, the fact that more than a few people have said that, means I'm probably pretty good.

Yet, here is this guy who tells me he sucks at advertising, crushing me in terms of ROI.

That's when I knew there was something to this whole high-ticket thing.

After that conversation, I spent the next year learning everything I could about high-ticket, phone sales, overcoming objections, managing a sales team, etc.

We then launched our first high-ticket program. Almost right away, I knew this was what was missing.

Almost everything was the same, except for a few key things.

First, instead of getting people to watch a webinar and asking them to buy on an order page, we asked them to book a call.

On this call, we would ask them a few questions about their situation. We would make sure our product could help solve their problem, and if it could, we would offer for them to join.

The very first month we did this, I spent $18,000 on advertising and made back $121,000 in sales.

If you know anything about online advertising, that's a pretty crazy return.

Not to mention, as we kept scaling, I noticed several things happening.

First, our ROI increased immediately, mainly because we were charging more.

Also, we didn't have to spend nearly as much on advertising to make the same amount of sales. We needed six people to buy our lower-ticket program to make the same amount of money as one person purchasing this high-ticket program.

So not only was the return on advertising higher, but we also didn't need to spend as much.

Far less staff were needed to attend to that product.

Yes, because there were fewer customers to serve, but more importantly, because of the quality of the customers. In my experience, the more money a customer pays you, the less needy they are.

This is the truth. Clients that have paid me $50,000 for consulting rarely, if ever, bother me with a silly request. But every time I would sell a $50 product, scores of support requests came in with silly questions.

Now I'm not hating on people that buy my lower-priced products. In fact, many of those people turn into higher-end clientele. I'm merely reporting to you what happens at different price points.

As well, refunds, chargebacks, and piracy virtually disappeared.

No one asked for a refund because they would have a 45-minute call with someone in my office before buying. They were sure it was a legitimate charge because the representative told them how it would appear on their credit card statement. They also were sure the product would solve their problem because they'd just spent nearly an hour making sure that it was a good fit, not an impulse buy.

Once they purchased, the representative would ensure they had their username and password. They would make sure they logged in and had everything they bought.

So 99% of the reason people ask for a refund was eliminated.

Next, let's look at chargebacks. Most chargebacks happen because of fraud or the customer not recovering login information.

There isn't much fraud when someone is on a recorded call with you, has identified themselves, gives you their card number, and signs a legal contract. You have to have a pretty big set of you-know-what to commit fraud with that process.

Let's recap thus far. There are virtually no refunds and no chargebacks. That's already cutting out a huge expense.

Next is piracy. People who commit online piracy are cowards, and cowards don't like to get on the phone. They tend to hide behind the veil of the internet and very rarely rear their disgusting heads in the real world.

The call is recorded, their IP address is recorded, and they sign a contract. It just doesn't happen.

We've sold over $3 million worth of that program as I write this book, and the program has not become a victim to pirating.

By switching to high-ticket, we made more return on our advertising budget, and eliminated much of the work in three departments, which allowed us to consolidate three departments into just one.

Now, I still have those departments because we do continue to sell lower-priced products, like the book you're holding in your hand.

But instead of two people in each department, we now only need one. This is due to the majority of our actual revenue coming from people buying our premium programs.

Imagine a multi-million dollar company where ONE person can handle three departments. That's insane. But insanely good!

So as you can see, high-ticket solves a lot of issues in this business by nature.

But there is one more thing that is more important than anything I've listed thus far.

When you charge more for your product or service, you now can increase the quality of said product.

Try selling something for $50 and offering a weekly coaching call. You will have hundreds and hundreds of people on the call, and will not be able to give any real value to one person.

Charge $5,000 or $10,000? Now you only have a couple dozen on the call and can take time to dive into people's individual issues on the calls.

You can also spend more money on developing the program because you're making way more income.

Need a new camera to film your videos? Need a more comfortable desk? Need a bigger office?

With low-ticket, those could become a real concern in your budget.

With high-ticket, just one sale could pay your entire office rent for the month.

Get another sale? That could pay for brand new office furniture.

Get another sale? That could pay for your next quarterly vacation.

Yes, I take a vacation every quarter. At least a week or more. I couldn't do that when I only focused on low-ticket. With high-ticket, there are fewer moving parts, fewer issues, far fewer staff members, and fewer problems. I can step away much more often.

Who wouldn't want to get paid more for what they do, while at the same time being able to provide much more value to their customers?

Who wouldn't want to make more impact while making more profit?

Now, there is one caveat to selling high-ticket. You must sell it over the phone.

That means, yes, you must get on a call and sell people. It also means that eventually, you'll have to hire salespeople and train them to close for you if you want to scale, and more importantly, enjoy those quarterly vacations!

Now, before you say to yourself, "That's out of the question for me! I hate sales!"

So do I. When I was younger, I used to make phone sales for a water softener company and DIRECTV, and I hated every minute of it.

Do you know what I hate more?

Managing thousands of support tickets, dealing with multiple refund requests, chargebacks, and so on.

I also really like working with higher-end clientele. Generally, the more people pay, the more serious they tend to be.

When I consider all of this, I can say without a shadow of a doubt: I made the right decision.

Managing a sales team can be time-consuming. But it is nowhere near as time-consuming as managing thousands of customers that buy cheap products, especially if that is ALL you offer.

That said, high-ticket is not for everyone. In fact, it will not apply to most people.

You may think high-ticket is not for you because you don't know enough, you don't have enough credibility, or you don't have enough value to give.

This is rarely the case. High-ticket is not about how much you know. It's about how much the solution to your customers' problem is worth to them. Most of the time, giving that customer more attention will get them a better result.

The reason high-ticket is not for most is that most people aren't willing to do what it takes to make it work.

It's not easy. But I love that. I love doing things that are hard because I know that most of my competitors won't be willing to do it, simply because it's hard. So by embracing something that may seem hard to others, I've already cut out 90% of my competition.

One of my clients, Andy, was only charging $2,000 for his program and was struggling to remain profitable. So after looking at his situation, I determined it would be worth giving high-ticket a go. I recommended that he more than double the price of his offer, as well as showed him how to adjust his marketing for high-ticket.

When he was charging the lower price, he was doing about

$25,000 per month. His profit was only $5,000. He was barely breaking even. After we converted his offer to high-ticket, he was able to hit $122,000 in a single month and is slowly growing each month! His sales not only went up, but so did his profit. Instead of barely breaking even, he ended up spending $60,000 to make $122,000. That's a $62,000 profit in a single month!

If you would like to see a case study and complete breakdown of everything we did to convert him to high-ticket, visit: **DigitalMillionaireSecrets.com/andy.**

THE REAL SECRET
OF SCALE

This chapter will be the shortest in the book.

As we come to the end of this section on scaling your offer, I'd like to let you know that the next section of this book will help you scale far more than the current one.

Many things help in scaling your education business. Sure, there are advertising tricks, software, systems, etc.

But those things, like the wind, change.

What doesn't change is your ability to focus, be productive, make good decisions, and above all, maintain a "Million Dollar Mindset."

As we all know, superheroes do not exist. There are no mutants with mind control powers.

Or are there?

Most people fail because they let their mind run away with itself. They get distracted, move from shiny object to shiny object, or make poor decisions.

The real villain in any entrepreneur's story is their mind.

Your ability to control your mind is the number one thing that will allow you to scale.

Some think that mind control powers mean you have the ability to control other people's minds. But I believe it's hard enough to control your own mind.

If you can control your own mind, I would consider that a superpower.

The next section of this book will teach you the closest thing to mind control powers that can exist in reality.

Developing
Mind Control

THE CIRCLE OF FOCUS

W̲hat do Bill Gates, Warren Buffet, and Steve Jobs have in common?

Unrelenting Focus.

According to an article in *Forbes* magazine, when Bill Gates Sr. asked his son Bill Gates Jr., the founder of Microsoft, and his other famous billionaire dinner guest, Warren Buffet, "What factor do you feel has been the most important in getting to where you've gotten in life?"[10]

Warren Buffet replied with a single word (and Bill Gates Jr. agreed):

"Focus."

Steve Jobs provides a little more context for what focus means to him:

> "People think focus means saying yes to the thing you've got to focus on. But that's not what it means at all. It means saying no to the hundred other good ideas that there are. You have to pick carefully. I'm actually as proud of the things we haven't done as the things I have done."[11]

Now I haven't made billions like these giants, but if you asked me the same question, I would give you the same answer.

But, maintaining focus is easier said than done. Mainly because I never quite had a battle plan when it came to focus. People would always say, "Just focus! Keep your eye on the prize."

I would think, "Yeah, thanks. That's super helpful."

So, let me introduce you to a concept that will help you. I discovered this when I hit my lowest month of sales in two years.

At the time, we hadn't had a month that dropped below $250,000 in almost three years. Our best month ever at that point was $360,000. The best part? I only had one product, a single online course.

Now you may think anyone should be happy with these numbers. But as an entrepreneur, it's our basic instinct to grow, as was mine. I wanted to grow.

Still being relatively young in the business, I decided if I wanted to make more money, I would need more products! I decided, instead of only running paid ads, I would branch out and expand my promotion efforts to other platforms and methods. I started blogging, podcasting, making videos, doing joint venture launches, etc.

Everyone else was doing this, so I decided to do it, too. However, as my father used to say, "If everyone jumped off a bridge, would you jump as well?" I wish my father would have told me that again on this day.

For the next six months, sales went down, down, down. I would make a small product, like a mini-course, and sell the crap out of it. The time, effort, and focus I put into that new product took away from my efforts in my main product. If I made an extra $50,000 from a new product, sales would drop $80,000 on our main program.

The problem was not only more products. It was also how we promoted. Prior to this, I only promoted through Facebook ads. As I started focusing on other platforms, blogging, podcasting, etc., things got worse. Half of the time, I didn't even finish executing whatever my plan was on a particular platform. The other half distracted me so much that my ads were performing nowhere near what they had been.

I was tired, burnt out, and was starting to think I was washed up. Yet, whenever I gave my clients advice, it worked. They had success. So how could I be washed up?

Well, it wasn't copywriting, advertising, marketing, or sales. I later found out, it was focus.

I knew I had to do something.

So I reached out to a fellow entrepreneur I had met previously online, Sam Ovens. See, Sam was is the same business as I was, but instead of doing what everyone else does and create product after product, promote on platform after platform, he did the opposite. He focused on scaling ONE product and promoting on ONE platform. This intrigued me, so I decided to attend his next mastermind meeting.

There were several people there that had also created 7-figure businesses, as well as some that hit 8-figures.

I assumed we would be talking about copy, ads, sales, things of that nature. But the majority of the event centered around diet, sleep, and focus.

To summarize, the main thing I got from the weekend was, focus on ONE thing. Master it. Master it so well that you can then delegate it. Not outsource it, *delegate* it. Then move on to the next thing.

I went home with a renewed sense of purpose, but I was still confused about how to implement. So I sat down at my desk and as I always do, and tried to map out my plan of action.

This was when I came up with "The Circle of Focus." This changed my life.

Once I drew out "The Circle of Focus," it forced me to make some significant changes. I simplified my company. I stopped advertising and marketing on all but one channel. I even deleted 90% of my products.

Now, this may sound like I signed my own company's death certificate. Not only did our sales rapidly return to normal but in February of 2019, we hit our first million dollar month.

It was not due to any specific marketing tactic, script, or gimmick.

It was purely due to focus.

Would you like to learn "The Circle of Focus"?

If you said YES in your head, then grab a piece of paper.

Draw a big circle on it, and somewhere inside the circle, write out something you are working on.

So let's say you are trying to grow an online course business. Write down, "Facebook Ads." Currently, how much of the circle is taken up by Facebook Ads? 100%.

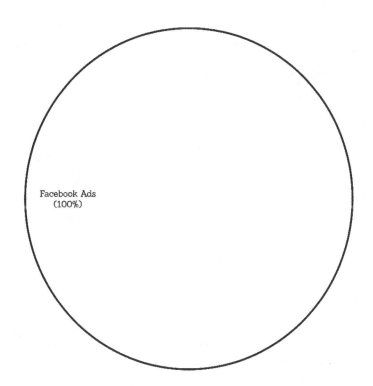

Now write down something else you are doing to promote your business.

"Podcast."

Now draw a line through the circle, separating the two.

It should look something like this:

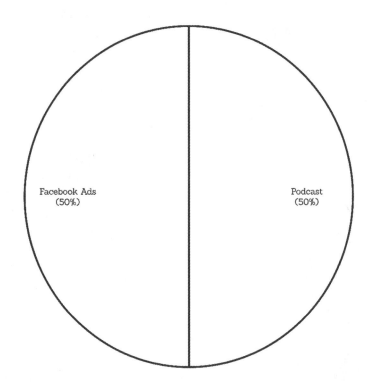

You will notice, instead of giving 100% effort to one thing, you are now giving 50% effort to two things.

When is the last time you heard of something succeeding by giving only 50% effort?

Now put in whatever else you are doing—blogging, guest posting, YouTube channel, etc.

Soon you will find your circle may look like a pizza. If it does, you are in trouble.

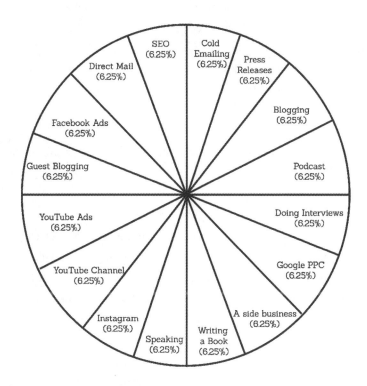

You'll find you may be giving only 5-10% effort on any one thing. How do you expect to grow a business giving 5-10% effort?

"But Dan, you have Facebook ads, YouTube ads, a book, etc."

Yes, I do. But, I focused and mastered each one until it became well-oiled—until it either barely took up my time, or I was able to train my staff to take it over. Only then did I move on to the next thing. If it was something I outsourced, I made sure to have ample time to focus on working with the person I hired to optimize and get the most out of it.

If you are thinking about starting a podcast, ask yourself if your current advertising system is fully built out. Or perhaps it's your email sequence. Is that done? Is it working and bringing you consistent money? Or are you still pulling your hair out over it? If YES, then you have no business starting a blog or podcast to get more traffic.

"But Dan, I think if I do this other thing, it will work better or be easier!"

This is called "Shiny Object Syndrome." If you can't focus enough to fix something that isn't working, how can you expect to get something else to work starting from square one? You can't. The same thing will happen over and over. You will move from thing to thing and get nowhere. If it's worked just ONCE for someone else, it can work for you. The difference between you and them? They were focused.

I'm not telling you this because it's my opinion. I'm telling you this because it's what I've seen going from zero to over 8-figures. It's also what I've heard dozens of billionaires say, and more millionaires than I can count.

So take your "Circle of Focus," and start deleting things. Pick the things that move the needle the most, find what works, and do more of that. Only do new things once the things you're working on are so refined that they are now boring to execute and easily managed by your staff.

I've seen people try to get an increase in traffic to their webinar by using a podcast. But at the same time, they haven't even finished their email sequence! It's madness!

"But Dan, I can multitask!"

I hate to break this to you, but multitasking is a lie.

Multitasking leads to a 40% decrease in productivity. This was determined by the The American Psychological Association.

Billionaire Mike Cannon-Brookes has mentioned it was only when he gave up multitasking that he was able to be truly productive.

Do one thing at a time. Period.

But in today's world, there are so many distractions. Social media, a tool that has made so many rich, has actually made many more poor.

Want to stay focused? Delete distractions. Remove all social media apps from your phone. Buy a second phone if you must to promote on social media, and keep it locked in a drawer until you need it.

Don't read your email. Delete it from your phone. I haven't read mine in two years. My assistant sorts through it daily and lets me know if anything requires my attention. No assistant? Set aside a 30-minute block every day to read your email. Don't respond to everyone, only those that warrant a response.

Stop agreeing to interviews, lunches, meetings, etc. They are a distraction.

Jacqueline Leo, the former Vice President of Reader's Digest, who has also won more awards for media publishing than Tom Brady has in championship rings, said, "One look at an email can rob you of 15 minutes of focus. One call on your cell phone, one tweet, one instant message can destroy your schedule, forcing you to move meetings, or blow off really important things, like love, and friendship."[12]

Mark Pincus, a billionaire and founder of the popular social video game Zynga, says, "not to accept speaking opportunities unless they directly benefit your customers or company. They are a waste of time."[13]

Have you ever heard of Lee Lacocca? He was the man that took Chrysler from almost closing the doors to one of the best years in its history. But after he had done this, he started spending a ton of time going on talk shows, TV shows, and doing interviews. Shortly thereafter, Chrysler's stock plunged.

Ego is a distraction.

Og Mandino, an American author who has sold over 50 million books, said, "It is those who concentrate on but one thing at a time who advance in this world."

The fewer things you have on your plate, the easier it will be to succeed at what's in front of you. Want to fail less? Do less. Focus more.

Keep your "Circle of Focus" clean.

"Focus is a matter of deciding what things you're not going to do."

— John Carmack

SLAYING THE HATERS

"To avoid criticism, do nothing, say nothing, be nothing."

— Elbert Hubbard

Whether you are doing something right or wrong, you will have haters. The only time you won't is if you do nothing at all.

If you say nothing, nobody can criticize you. If you do nothing, nobody can criticize you. However, if you say nothing and do nothing, you will be nothing.

Another great quote is by Matthew Stevenson: "You will never be criticized by someone doing more than you. You will be criticized by someone doing less."

It's natural to be worried about criticism once you proclaim yourself an expert or an authority on a specific subject. I've had thousands of comments from people on social media saying horrible things about me. Every time I launch a new ad, there are always negative comments. I've even had someone send me a message that said, "I wish your baby died in the hospital."

Yet, we have over 15,000 customers. That's 15,000 people that liked what I had to say. They liked it so much that they decided to give me their hard-earned money to hear more.

Aileen, one of my clients who is now a 7-figure earner, once asked me, "Dan, how do you deal with people saying bad things about you? I get so frustrated!"

I then asked about her clients. I asked how many people's lives she had changed. She told me story after story of women she has helped grow their photography businesses.

So I said, "Whose opinion do you care about more? Those who made a passing judgment because they were bored? Or those who listened and had enough faith to pay you?"

"Point made," she replied.

Judge yourself not by what people say about you, but by how many pay you. I never look at Facebook comments as a measure of how well I am doing. I look at my sales.

If you are doing a lousy job, then people either won't buy at all or the people that do buy, will give you feedback. Trust me.

I've never seen a negative comment, clicked on the person's profile, and read they were a billionaire. Usually, they are un-employed. Warren Buffet is not going to send me a message and say, "Dan, you suck."

Do not take what those people say and let it bother you because it makes no sense to let it aggravate you.

Now, if someone says, "I think it's a scam because of this specific reason." Well, maybe you should pay attention to that and adjust your marketing if needed. That's an entirely different story.

But if things are selling, everything's going great, and people are criticizing you, sending you mean messages, then it doesn't matter!

If what other people said mattered, they wouldn't have time to say it.

But wait! What if it's YOU that is the one saying mean things about yourself? What if you have the dreaded "Imposter Syndrome"?

In my opinion, the easiest way to get over "Imposter Syndrome" is to build things that matter.

So if you say to yourself, "I can't do this because I have Imposter Syndrome." Well, the simple act of doing it is how you get over it. If you build something that matters, you won't have "Imposter Syndrome" because you'll have built something great.

What if you have no credibility? First, you must realize that credibility is all about perception.

Do you know what Christopher Nolan, Stanley Kubrick, Quentin Tarantino, and Steven Spielberg all have in common? They never went to film school.

If you build something that matters, that's credibility. If your students are getting results, that's credibility.

I read an article once about a guy that made a million dollars selling a course on how to make money on eBay. He only makes $500 a week from selling on eBay. People want that $500 a week, that's good enough for them, and he's able to teach them and get the results they desire. He made a promise, not a big one, but one that he can fulfill.

You don't have to be rich to teach a business course. You don't have to be Mr. Olympia to teach a fitness course. You don't have to be a famous actor to teach an acting course.

Credibility is about perception, and your only perception should be your students' results.

"You are the worst pirate I've ever heard of!"

*"Ah, but you **have** heard of me!"*

— Captain Jack Sparrow

Why People Don't Buy Your Stuff

H ave you ever wondered why people don't buy your stuff?

For seven years, I barely made a penny online. Then, out of nowhere, I became an overnight success.

People have asked me over the years what shift I made that created the difference. I never could really pinpoint it until I met Myron Golden.

I was invited to speak at an event held in Orlando by another well-known internet entrepreneur, Dana Derricks. The event, like most, was structured to give amazing value to the crowd for three days, and then make an offer for a high-ticket program.

I arrived, thinking there would be a couple hundred people. To my surprise, there were only about 15. What I didn't realize? The tickets were $2,000 to attend! So the event was more of an intimate setting.

I'm sure they made a decent profit on just ticket sales, but I knew they were going to make another offer at the end of the event. I remember thinking, "How is Dana going to make any money?!?! There are only 15 people here!"

That was until I saw Myron speak—and generate $150,000 in sales in this tiny room of 15 people.

It was at that moment I knew I had to know this guy.

I introduced myself, and before I could get a word out, Myron started complimenting me on my speech. He was the nicest, most cordial person I had ever met in my life. When he spoke, he wasn't pushy; in fact, he was the furthest thing from a high-pressure salesman.

A few weeks later, I invited Myron to my home for dinner. We talked all night, and I told him my story. I told him how in the beginning, I spent money I didn't have on my business. I would eat ramen noodles all week, so I could instead spend my money on books, courses, and software. Once I had some success, I bought into multiple $30,000+ masterminds to further my knowledge.

At one point, Myron said to me, "Do you know why you are successful?"

"A lot of reasons, I guess, but do you see something I'm not seeing?"

Over the next 30 minutes, Myron enlightened me.

He pointed out the fact that I had spent hundreds of thousands of dollars on my own education. I wanted to build a huge business selling my advice online. Ironically, my road to success included paying a great deal to others for their advice.

He explained that successful entrepreneurs view spending money as investments. Unsuccessful entrepreneurs view spending money as an expense.

You sell like you buy.

If you can't bring yourself to pay a premium price for a solution to your problem, you will never be able to ask someone else to pay a premium price for your solution to their problem.

There will be too much internal conflict. It will come through on your calls, your marketing, your emails—everything you put out.

Remember that old adage, "You are your friends?" Well, it's true, and so is this next one. "You get what you are."

If you never invest in yourself, you will attract customers that never invest either. If you continuously invest in yourself, you will attract those that do the same.

Myron really opened my eyes that night. Even though I had followed those principles, it was of great value to understand why.

Here is a perfect example. When we started selling high-ticket, I had a massive problem with my sales team. Their close rates were low, and I was struggling to find time to review their calls and give them advice on how to improve.

So I reached out to a friend of mine named Molly.

Molly was running a high-ticket business selling a program on how to make money as a boudoir photographer, which was pretty cool considering boudoir photography can be much more lucrative than wedding photography. A fact I wasn't aware of, but I can see why her program did so well!

She had several salespeople that were crushing it, and she'd been doing this for a while.

So I reached out to ask her if I could pay to have her review my sales team's calls and give them some advice.

She declined, stating she didn't have the time. That was until I offered to pay her $1,000 per hour. Once she heard that, she gladly accepted.

At the same time, I reached out to one of the top salespeople that worked for a colleague of mine. I gave her the same offer.

About $10,000 later, my sales team had received several videos through email going over their calls and giving them suggestions.

The very next week, their close rates spiked up dramatically.

We even closed an extra $50,000 in sales over the next two weeks. Compared to the month prior, we had increased our sales by $80,000 for that product.

So you could hear the story one of two ways. Either you hear it as, "Dan spent $10,000 just to have someone listen to some calls?"

Or you could hear it as, "Dan spent $10,000 to make $80,000 back, and he gets to make more money every month after that as well!"

I could never meet you and never speak to you. But, based on which story you chose above, I could tell you how likely you are to be a successful entrepreneur.

Tony Robbins said, "Find somebody that is successful at what you want to do, model what they are doing, and you will be successful."

While I agree with Tony, I prefer to speed things up a bit. You can try to figure out what someone else is doing, model them, and even copy them. But without seeing behind the scenes, you are missing 90% of the recipe.

For example, one time I was testing a new strategy in my business that ended up not working out. It only lasted for about a week before we stopped using it because it was completely ineffective.

About a month later, I saw this guy charging $47 for a training on how to do what I was doing. He was claiming he had studied this strategy I was using and was able to reverse engineer it, breaking down each part of the strategy in vivid detail.

For fun, I bought this guy's training, and not only did he get most of what I did wrong, but the whole strategy didn't work anyway. And he had sold hundreds of copies of this training! The whole time, he and his customers thought this strategy was effective, and it wasn't. There is a reason we have the saying, "The blind leading the blind." This was a perfect example.

Do you see why it's a terrible idea to try to copy someone without knowing what's going on behind the scenes?

There's a better, faster way to model success.

Find that successful person. Pay that person whatever they want to show you exactly how they are doing it.

That's the fastest way to success.

You can't buy love, but you can buy success.

THE MATRIX AND THE MARTIAN

Have you ever seen the movie *The Matrix*?

I'm sure you have. But in case you haven't, it was a movie about how everyone in the world is plugged into a computer simulation called "The Matrix." The real world is a barren wasteland full of human pods, harvesting our bodies for electricity while we sleep and live in this virtual world.

In the movie, there is a resistance group that unplugs people from the Matrix, rescuing them from the world they think is real.

When the movie begins, we find it centered around a new recruit named "Neo," played by Keanu Reeves. Neo is discovered to be "The Chosen One," or as they call him in the movie, "The One."

"The One" is supposed to have powers far-reaching beyond anyone else in the movie. Neo is essentially their Superman equivalent.

Everyone removed from the Matrix goes through a simulated training program. One of the simulations has recruits attempt to jump from one building to the next. This feat is impossible in the real world, but as long as you know how to manipulate your mind, it is doable in the Matrix.

However, no one has ever made the first jump. Recruits always fall the first time, and it takes several attempts before they gain enough faith to make the jump.

Several members of the resistance group think that Neo will make the first jump because he is the chosen one.

However, when Neo attempts his very first jump, like everyone else, he falls. Some members of the resistance think this is normal because everyone falls. Others think it means he might not be "The One."

Spoiler alert! The prophecy is accurate, and Neo becomes "The One." He takes on hundreds of opponents at the same time, can fly, and even shows supernatural powers outside of the Matrix.

Yet, even though he is the most powerful character in the story, he still falls in his first attempt.

See, we all fall. Do you think Michael Jordan was amazing at shooting hoops the first time he touched a basketball? Do you think Tiger Woods could drive 300 yards the first time he picked up a golf club?

You will not get this right the first time. No one ever has. Accept this as part of the process, and you'll get much farther much faster. Frustration is a byproduct of progress, just as being sore is a byproduct of working out. If you stop working out just because you get sore, you'll never get fit.

As we bring this book to its conclusion, you might be thinking...

"This sounds hard."

Well, I'll be honest with you. Entrepreneurship can be hard. But so can working for a boss that doesn't appreciate you, 40 hours per week, for the rest of your life. That's harder.

Many have asked how I would summarize entrepreneurship. I didn't have a good answer until I saw the movie, *The Martian* with Matt Damon.

In the movie, Matt Damon plays astronaut Mark Watney, whose specialty is botany.

Mark's team travels to Mars, and when they leave, something goes wrong, and he ends up getting stranded on Mars.

Because they only had a certain amount of fuel, the only way to rescue him was to go back to Earth, re-fuel, and come back to get him.

This predicament left him having to figure out how to survive on a barren desert planet for over a year.

Because Mark was a botanist, he was able to figure out how to generate enough moisture on Mars to grow potatoes. He rationed them out to consume just enough to keep himself alive. Multiple times, he faced problem after problem that seemed to guarantee his fate.

As difficult as this sounds, he never gave up. He was able to stay alive until they rescued him and delivered him safely back to

Earth. He weighed around 100 pounds when they rescued him, but he made it!

At the end of the movie, we move forward a couple of decades in time. We see Mark teaching a group of aspiring astronauts.

What he says to them will stick with me for the rest of my life.

> *"At some point, everything's gonna go south on you... everything's going to go south and you're going to say, this is it. This is how I end. Now you can either accept that, or you can get to work. That's all it is. You just begin. You do the math. You solve one problem... and you solve the next one... and then the next. And if you solve enough problems, you get to come home.."[14]*
>
> *— Mark Watney, The Martian*

When I heard that quote, my entire entrepreneurial journey made sense.

When you begin your journey as an entrepreneur, you have a goal. As you move toward that goal, you are faced with problems.

If you get frustrated and stop solving problems, your business dies. But if you solve enough problems, you get to become a millionaire.

How to Get
MORE HELP

YOUR FREE TICKET

If there's one thing I love to do, it's teach people how to replicate my success. So, in addition to the short bonus training videos included in this book, I've also included a special one-hour training that shows you exactly how I grew a multi-million dollar online education business.

If you enjoyed this book, you will love this training. It walks you through many of the strategies mentioned in this book in greater detail.

Visit **DigitalMillionaireSecrets.com/ticket** to watch that training now.

I can't guarantee how long I will keep this training up as I do rotate and update training frequently. But for now, it's there. I suggest you take advantage.

DigitalMillionaireSecrets.com/ticket

How to Access
Your Bonuses

Sprinkled throughout this book are several free bonuses. These are training videos hosted on our website to accompany the content in this book.

You'll see the links to the videos included throughout the chapters; however, here is a list of each one mentioned in the book for quick reference.

Free Webinar: How to Start and Grow a Profitable Online Course Business

This one-hour training covers how we built a multi-million dollar education business. This training goes over many strategies mentioned in this book in greater detail.

Access at: DigitalMillionaireSecrets.com/ticket

Our Webinar Script

This video training covers our current webinar script and framework. We have used this script to generate over $10 million in sales, and more importantly, to show our clients how to convert their message into a sellable format. Many of our clients have made 7-figures with this script. Enjoy.

Access at: DigitalMillionaireSecrets.com/script

Our On-Demand Webinar System

This video breaks down the current system and funnel we use to deliver our webinar to prospects and convert them to paying customers.

Access at: DigitalMillionaireSecrets.com/system

The Goldfish Rule In Action

This is a collection of several examples of our successful advertisements that follow The Goldfish Rule (getting to the point within nine seconds).

Access at: DigitalMillionaireSecrets.com/goldfish

High-Ticket Case Study

This is a video interview with one of our clients who transitioned from a low-ticket product to a high-ticket one, taking him from break-even to extremely profitable 6-figure months.

Access at: DigitalMillionaireSecrets.com/andy

Client Results

If you are curious about what kind of results one can expect from implementing our strategies, I've compiled some screenshots from just a few of our premium clients, celebrating their wins. Feel free to check these out to inspire you towards what's possible.

Access at: DigitalMillionaireSecrets.com/success

Beta Success

As mentioned in the book, many of our clients experience success by pre-selling a program before they create it. This is also known as a Beta Launch. I've compiled a few "Beta Success" examples from our clients.

Access at: DigitalMillionaireSecrets.com/beta

Speak to Us

If you would like some help from my team implementing the strategies in the book and ultimately growing your online education business, we'd like to invite you to speak to us.

Head over to **DigitalMillionaireSecrets.com/speak**.

There will be a short application asking a few questions about your business or your business idea. (So we can review them before the call).

Answer the questions, and on the next page, you'll see a calendar with a list of available dates and times for your call. Pick the one that works best for you.

Once you have booked your time, the confirmation page will have some instructions on how to prepare for the call. Please review them thoroughly. Watch the video that breaks down what it looks like to work with us. Review the case studies from our clients. That way, when you get on the call, you will already have quite a few of your questions answered.

Once on the call, my office will take a look at what you are doing, identify the problems you're having, and see if we can help. If we can help, we will show you what it looks like to work with us. You can then decide if you want to become one of our clients or not.

No pressure, but either way, you will get a lot of clarity out of this call.

Visit **DigitalMillionaireSecrets.com/speak** to book your call today.

REFERENCES

1. TJ McCue, "E Learning Climbing To $325 Billion By 2025 UF Canvas Absorb Schoology Moodle," Forbes.com, July 31, 2018. https://www.forbes.com/sites/tjmccue/2018/07/31/e-learning-climbing-to-325-billion-by-2025-uf-canvas-absorb-schoology-moodle/#639ddae83b39.

2. Mark Watney [from deleted scene], *The Martian*. 2015. Directed by Ridley Scott. Twentieth Century Fox, https://www.imdb.com/title/tt3659388/characters/nm0000354#quotes.

3. Sun Tzu, *The Art of War,* trans. Lionel Giles, first published 1910, (Los Angeles: Enhanced Media, 2017).

4. Russell Brunson, *Expert Secrets: The Underground Playbook to Find Your Message, Build a Tribe, and Change the World,* (New York: Morgan James, 2017), 88.

5. Justin Kazmark, "Kickstarter Before Kickstarter," Kickstarter.com. July 18, 2013. https://www.kickstarter.com/blog/kickstarter-before-kickstarter?fbclid=IwAR0XPfyDpA_VGoT_yRzy7gbSt8sVXrN43rA7tZH-mwkDxHMr4GFVAnri0O0.

6. Steven James Snyder, "Kickstarter: The 50 Best Inventions of 2010," Time.com, November 11, 2010. http://content.time.com/time/specials/packages/article/0,28804,2029497_2030652_2029823,00.html.

7. Perry Chen, "Our Story," Kickstarter.com. https://www.kickstarter.com/press?ref=about_subnav&fbclid=IwAR338uIOF4n6yVwYHy8-

KbDKx8RrQiJQESQaqo3IAztAYnJTDuR23g7KzEs#th
e-full-story, accessed December 16, 2019.

8. Kickstarter, PBC. Kickstarter.com.
   https://www.kickstarter.com/help/stats?ref=press,
   accessed December 15, 2019.

9. Kevin McSpadden, "You Now Have a Shorter Attention
   Span Than a Goldfish," Time.com, May 14, 2015.
   https://time.com/3858309/attention-spans-goldfish/.

10. Rainer Zitelmann, "What Focus Really Means: Learning
    From Bill Gates, Warren Buffett And Steve Jobs,"
    Forbes.com, October 28, 2019.
    https://www.forbes.com/sites/rainerzitelmann/2019/10/2
    8/what-focus-really-means-learning-from-bill-gates-
    warren-buffett-and-steve-jobs/#586b634173fc.

11. Ibid.

12. Jacqueline Leo Quotes. BrainyQuote.com, BrainyMedia
    Inc, 2019.
    https://www.brainyquote.com/quotes/jacqueline_leo_54
    7986, accessed December 13, 2019.

13. Mark Pincus Quote. Will Chou, "How Self-made
    Billionaires Prioritize for Better Focus and
    Productivity," Medium.com, February 9, 2016.
    https://medium.com/better-marketing/10-billionaire-
    productivity-hacks-that-will-save-you-years-of-time-
    3b2f14ceec8.

14. Mark Watney [last lines], *The Martian*. 2015. Directed
    by Ridley Scott. Twentieth Century Fox,
    https://www.imdb.com/title/tt3659388/characters/nm000
    0354#quotes.

ABOUT THE AUTHOR

Dan Henry started his first company to pay his way through college. His first efforts, while only mildly successful, inspired him to drop out of college and pursue entrepreneurship full time.

Since then, he has sold over $10 million of his own products online, grown a massive following, and has been featured in *Forbes*, *Entrepreneur Magazine*, *Business Insider,* and more.

Dan took what he learned from this journey, founded GetClients.com, and helped thousands of entrepreneurs turn their dreams into reality. This includes being instrumental in the creation of several millionaires without VC funding, JV partnerships, and zero following.

His motto is, "Some people teach you what to do and how to do it. I teach you how to do it well."